WHAT IF IT'S
Time for a Change

Skinny Book™

By:

Jackie Woodside, CPC, LICSW

ISBN: 978-0-9853555-4-8

Published by Portrait Health Publishing, Inc.
2201 Waukegan Road, Suite 170, Bannockburn, IL 60015
www.portraithealthpublishing.com

Cover Design by Jeremy Shape

Disclaimer

DEDICATION

Upon the apt advice of my seven-year-old son, this book is dedicated to the Spirit of God, Who makes all things possible. Thank you, Nathan, for your Wisdom and Knowing...

...and to the hundreds of clients and students that I have known and loved over the past 25 years who have graciously invited my presence on their paths to change.

TABLE OF CONTENTS

ACKNOWLEDGEMENTS

It is a wonderful experience in life to watch one's dreams manifest into reality. This book is just that – a dream manifest before me. For as long as I can remember, I have wanted to write and publish my thoughts on so many topics in life. I wrote plays and stories as a child, filled countless journals as a young adult and to this very day. Yet the actual completion of a published book remained elusive for me until meeting the wonderful folks at Portrait Health Publishing.

I would thus like to thank Henry "Hank" Warner for seeing something in me despite our rather pronounced differences, and "trusting his gut" on our ability to form a solid, engaging and productive relationship. His right hand (or perhaps right brain!) is Dr. Jack Maggiore who stepped into this project with willingness and an open mind. His unwavering commitment to producing a work of the highest order of professional excellence was evident throughout the writing and editing of this book. Finally, Jeremy Warner provided the technical savvy, light-spirit and forward thinking to support the completion of this work. You are all very dear to me, and I cannot thank you enough for this process. What fun we have had!

Those who are blessed with an eye for detail are truly God's angels! I have been blessed with two lovely angels along my writing path. I would like to express a multitude of thanks to Kay Harker and Maria Alma Navedo for your editing work, keen eye, perceptive questions and tireless commitment to helping me along the way.

I would be remiss not to acknowledge the whole-hearted love and support I get from my family. There is nothing more precious than a home filled with love – and that is what I am blessed to experience each and every day.   Thank you, my beloveds.

Introduction

I sleep in the bed that belonged to my great grandparents. It was handcrafted in the 1800s. My grandmother and father were conceived in that bed. It is made of beautiful dark wood and displays ornate carvings along the head and footboard. There are old wooden slats that hold the mattress upon which I sleep. That bed has been around longer than anyone on the earth right now. It is sturdy and strong. I somehow feel cradled and protected in my family lineage sleeping in it.

Similarly, I spend my summers in the cottage that was built by my great aunt and uncle, in the town in which I was raised. My cousin took over the cottage when my great aunt Kitty died back in 1999 and then he passed it on to me when he could no longer maintain it the way he wanted. He hadn't changed much about the old, musty cottage when he was the owner, and now that it's mine, I find that I loathe changing much as well. There is an odd comfort in the familiarity of leaving things the way that they have been since before I was born. My great aunt and uncle's furnishings, blankets, pictures, books, dishes and pans surround me like a menagerie of old friends. I've walked up and down the lane leading up to this cottage my entire life and know every turn and bend in the road. The depth of connection I feel with this place comforts me like a warm blanket on a cold winter's evening.

What is it about the familiar that soothes our hearts and minds so dearly? I'm sure many of you reading this book can resonate with places and belongings that bring you this same sense of continuity and stability as my great grandparents' bed and my great aunt's cottage.

We say that we are creatures of habit, and I suppose this is true. Habits, routines and all-things-familiar help us to stay on an even keel, to feel a sense of predictability and control in an often-challenging and unpredictable world. So what happens when we are faced with change – either that which we have chosen and designed or that which is thrust upon us? How do we respond so that we maintain our resiliency and zest for life?

Buddhists say that all things are impermanent and that our desperate yearning for things to stay the same causes suffering. Predating Buddha is the Greek philosopher, Heraclitus who coined the phrase, "The only thing that stays the same is change." This line has been in country song lyrics, on bumper stickers and in all sorts of philosophy lessons. It is true. Impermanence is a fact of life and if we want to live in greater harmony and happiness, learning to master change must be part of our journey.

We live in a culture that is not entirely hospitable to those who are facing change. It almost seems that people think being around loss or upheaval might somehow mysteriously bring it on. We are expected to buck up, keep a stiff upper lip and get through it. Moreover, this attitude is seen as a virtue! We admire those who put their heads down and muddle through the twists and turns of life without uttering a word, a complaint, and heaven forbid a sadness or fear! I once had a therapy client who was grieving the loss of her husband. She returned to work after a few weeks away and reported feeling like people were avoiding her like she had some odd contagious illness, not experiencing grief. When she confided in one colleague that she was having difficulty adjusting to her husband's loss that she couldn't bring herself to give away his belongings, or even move his razor from the bathroom, her colleague's abrupt reply was along the lines of, "Shouldn't you be getting on with your life now?" That was less than a month after her husband's passing.

Change impacts us on so many levels. We are often left feeling adrift at sea without a compass to guide us. Resisting change creates a complex maze of inner conflict that crowds your psyche and smothers your spirit. This book is intended to be a primer on how to master, or at least learn to embrace change. The message of this book is simple and hopefully comforting: life will change, your body will change, your family will change, in fact, everything will change, and that is the true gift being human – to be awake and aware of what you cherish, present to the current moment and flowing with the beautiful, miraculous, and sometimes painful rhythms of life.

Throughout the book, we will examine different types of changes that we face and then look at *The Problem with Change* – why and how it impacts our lives and our psyche so dramatically. Then we will look at the fact that some people are simply more resilient to change. You will begin to understand your own personal *Change Temperament* and how to best face change given your particular change temperament. Lastly, we will explore the most important change of all – your perspective.

It is my hope that you will be left feeling both comforted and inspired to confront whatever change you are facing and those changes that lie ahead with a sense of clarity and power. You will know that you are not alone in your experience of change, that there is nothing "wrong" with you and that change and our various responses to it are a vital and important part of the human journey.

Chapter One: The Different Types of Change

A. The Types of Changes We Face and How We Respond to Them

By the time you finish reading this sentence something will have changed. Thousands of changes have occurred in the world, maybe millions of things have changed in the universe and at least a few things have changed in your own body. Things are changing all the time – grass is growing, children are learning, adults are aging, wars are beginning or ending, technology is expanding, currency is rising or falling. Our moods change by the day or even by the hour. Our bodies change despite our opinions and protestations about it. Change is endless and pervasive and those changes that directly impact our lives are the ones that get our attention.

One of the biggest adjustments of this generation is not the prevalence of change but tremendous rapidity of change. The changes we have seen occur in our lifetime are mind blowing and continue to accelerate every year. The advent of the technological and information age has been a game-changer for those trying to stay on top of the social and cultural landscape. I want to add a few examples of the technology we are now using and incorporating in our daily lives that were not even a thought a decade ago, but I fear that by the time this book goes to print, the technology items I may choose will be obsolete! So I will leave it to you to fill in the blank here – you are fully aware of the technology and information coming at you daily, hourly, and the ways in which you incorporate it (or try to!) into your life experience.

All of this is to say that in many ways we have become incredibly adept at adapting to change. And yet, in other ways, the pace and acceleration of change is bringing us to our knees.

In order to better understand the impact of change on our lives, we need to fully understand the types of change that we are dealing with and the variety of ways these changes impact us. When thinking about change, there are essentially four types of change that occur in our lives. These are 1) sudden planned change, 2) sudden unplanned change, 3) gradual planned change or 4) gradual unplanned change.

Let's look at each of these categories more closely so we can begin locating ourselves with regard to our own life changes.

Sudden, unplanned changes are accidents, unexpected promotions at work, being fired or laid off, winning the lottery or some other prize, unexpected breakups, the sudden death of a loved one or friend, acts of violence. Sudden, unplanned changes often create the greatest disequilibrium because we are unprepared and can feel powerless and victimized by the loss or change. Even sudden changes that are wonderful, positive experiences such as winning the lottery launch us on such a new and different path that it takes significant readjusting to incorporate the change. These changes can impact our most fundamental psychic structure – our level of consciousness or how we view the world. When we experience sudden, unplanned change that we deem as negative (i.e. acts of violence, loss, illness) we may come to see the world as inhospitable and malevolent, at least for a time. Similarly, experiencing a sudden change that we deem to be positive (unexpected winning, cash windfall and the like) we may come to see the world as benevolent and working in our favor. These changes in our perception of the world most often do not last. Yet there are times when an event is so powerful that it is truly life altering, changing our fundamental outlook on life.

Sudden, planned changes often have a significant impact on our lives, but we at least feel as though we have had control and choice in the change process. I remember when I left full-time employment for self-employment back in 1994. I felt so empowered by my choice and felt I was going out to carve and create my own career. It was a planned change, but there certainly was a given day that I went from employed to no-longer-employed by an external entity. With my final day as an employee, there was a sudden shift in my identity and sense of safety and belonging in the world. There were elements of this change that I could not have predicted and that only became apparent to me when the change had occurred. The day had come, I was no longer employed and it scared me to death! There was no going back. I could not undo what I had done and I felt terribly alone. My sense of confidence and adventure quickly turned into fear and uncertainty.

Gradual, planned changes are often more palatable and gentle to our psyche and spirit. Human nature is not inclined for change. We are creatures of habit, lovers of routine. Not many people wake up in the morning thinking, "I hope something totally new and unpredictable happens today!" That is just not how we are made. We are comforted by routine and feel safer when our world is predictable. So when thinking about any change process, gradual, planned change can be your best friend.

Success in any endeavor is often a process of gradual, planned change. If you have known anyone who was dubbed an "overnight success", I'm certain that you saw him or her work day and night on his or her field of endeavor before turning into the so-called "overnight success." The author and speaker Eckhart Tolle jokes about his rise as an internationally acclaimed thought leader. He laughs at the media claiming that he "rose from obscurity" and wonders where he was that was so obscure. Of course it is never the case that someone just emerges into a given field to achieve success, it is a process of slow, gradual change, and often a lot of hard work.

Gradual, unplanned changes can be so insidious that they become like a cancer in our lives. These are the ones that occur when we go unconscious in how we are living our lives, caring for our bodies, relationships, homes, cars and families. It is the extra 30 pounds that mysteriously shows up around your waist, or the quiet, yet uncomfortable distance that has occurred between you and your spouse or you and your kids. It can be the extra drink, and then two that you start having in the evenings, that over time add up to a drinking problem that you cannot understand how or where it began. Gradual, unplanned changes are the closets that are overflowing, the stacks of paper that have sat untouched for years, the spare room that is teeming with old and forgotten stuff. These all are examples of unplanned gradual changes that are the result of going unconscious in life. Not unconscious because we are uncaring or unhealthy, not because we didn't have dreams and goals at one time, but unconscious because we simply got caught up in the living of life. Gradual, unplanned changes occur when we forget who we are and what we want our lives to look like.

Table 1 provides a brief summary of some of the life transitions that fall into each of these four categories.

Table 1. Change Categories and Examples of Life Transitions

Category of Change	Example
Sudden, planned change: While the event has been planned, the actual change often comes up suddenly and there is a distinct, sudden moment that the change has taken place.	Home sale Relocation Job change Retirement Graduation Marriage Planned pregnancy
Sudden, unplanned change: Event is not planned, and there is a sudden, distinct moment that the change event has taken place.	Accident Illness Death of a loved one Windfall of money (lottery, investments, inheritance) Act of violence Relational break up Being fired from a job Eviction from a rental home or office Car breaks down Unplanned pregnancy
Gradual, planned change: There is not a single event that demarcates one moment of change. The change is gradual, there are specific actions that cause it, and it occurs over time.	Weight loss New exercise or self-care routine Any new goal, skill or hobby Travel or vacations Home renovations or building
Gradual, unplanned change: There is not a single event that demarcates the change. The change is gradual and unconscious (i.e. not in one's conscious awareness) over time.	Weight gain Loss of physical strength, flexibility and wellness Relationships wane or become unhealthy Loss of interest in career Loss of contemporary skills in career Development of an addiction Clutter and disorganization

When seeking to create an optimal outcome for yourself and your life, incorporating skilled elements of planned, gradual change is the path that will create the greatest success with the least difficulty. Let's face it, most of us do not seek out nor easily embrace change. Given this common human condition, it behooves us to learn and incorporate the elements of successful, stress-less change. These elements will be covered in the final chapter of this book, so for those of you who just want the answer to how to create planned, sustained, gradual change, just skip to the last chapter! However, failing to have a solid foundation of understanding of the multi-faceted elements of change may get in your way. Transition and change are huge topics in our lives and something we will be dealing with literally to the day we die. It may be well worth the investment to broaden your knowledge on the elements of change.

B. Change vs. Transition

The concepts of transition and change are often used interchangeably. The fact that we use these two words as synonyms points to the difficulty we have facing and embracing the reality of change, because they are two very different parts of a process. The full change/transition process includes the following elements: anticipation, change, adaptation, integration and resolution.

1. Change

Let's begin with the actual change as that is the most concrete and easily pinpointed of these five elements of the transition. Change is the event – the beginning of a new job, the move to a new state, beginning a graduate degree, marriage, bringing home a new child, the news that you are fired, the accident that leaves you seriously injured and needing to rehabilitate your body and so on. Change is the new thing that has occurred or that you must incorporate into your life.

We all face changes in every area and stage of our lives so you already have a great deal of experience in this topic! Congratulations! You have mastered going from the womb, to crawling, to walking to riding a bike to (probably) driving a car. There is a good chance that you successfully navigated the change of leaving high school, moving out of your parents' home, starting or ending a romance or two and completing an advanced degree. You have already mastered some, and probably many areas of life change. And yet you are reading this book which points to the fact that despite your advanced experience with the topic, there is still something about life change that leaves you baffled and perhaps a bit afraid. You want to feel like you "do" change better, understand it more fully and can master what life brings your way. There is an irony to this feeling – that somehow knowing more or understanding better will make change easier. There is some truth to that. Knowledge gives us power when facing uncertainty, but *knowledge applied* gives us wisdom, and it is wisdom that leads to peace in the face of emotional turmoil. The more we prepare for change, the better off we will be when change comes our way – either as an invited guest or an unwelcomed intruder. The first part of preparing for change is to understand the difference between the change event and the transition process.

If change is the actual event, then transition is the process that includes the actual change event, but also precedes and follows the event. Transition is the emotional and psychological adaptation to the new situation or circumstance you are incorporating into your life. The elements of the transition relate to your inner experience and adjustments in your relationships as a result of the external change. Let's look at each of these elements so you begin to understand what you may be experiencing at each stage of the change and transition process.

2. Anticipation

Anticipation is your emotional state prior to and in relation to the pending change. It is how you feel about the coming change, as well as what you say to yourself and others – which of course is indicative of how you feel about it. Common feelings associated with anticipation generally include the range of emotion spanning from excitement to anxiety. There is a phrase used by mental health clinicians known as "anticipatory anxiety" which is one's fear response to an upcoming planned change that results in psychological distress. Anticipatory anxiety may result in difficulty sleeping, heightened sensitivity, thoughts racing, feeling stressed and a general sense of overwhelm or even dread.

Anticipation also includes what you do as you engage in planned change. It may mean packing up your home in anticipation of your pending move, wrapping up your work as you prepare to leave one job for a new one, buying new clothes as you plan an extended vacation and so on. These activities are activities in anticipation of a planned change.

Going back to my example from 1994 when I left my job for self-employment, after I announced my new plans I remember everyone telling me how much courage I had and how brave I was. I remember feeling somewhat confused by this because it seemed to me that I was merely following a dream and that it would come to me as easily and naturally as getting the job in the first place. I was focusing on the CHANGE – going from employment, which felt cumbersome and restrictive to me, to self-employment, which felt freeing and liberating. So my period of ANTICIPATION was positive, excited, and expectant, filled with possibility.

Little did I know that I also had to go through each of the stages of the transition – which included developing a new identity, the loss of my sense belonging to that workplace group, and my sense of safety and being "taken care of" by that paycheck at the end of every week. I could not foresee those intangible but ever-so-powerful emotional reactions that were waiting for me the moment that change was complete. That is the difference between change and transition. Change occurs, and then we go through whatever myriad of emotional, psychological and spiritual reactions to that change. It is the transition that often causes us difficulty and pain.

3. Adaptation

Immediately after the change occurred and I left my job, my period of adaptation began. In the adaptation phase, the task is to assimilate the new circumstance or event into one's lifestyle and new view of life. The adaptation phase is probably the most difficult of all of the phases because it is the most active phase in which we are processing a great deal of new information and developing a new identity. By new identity, I mean the things that we use to label or identify ourselves. For example, I am a mother. I have the identity of someone who is a mother, which includes thoughts about my child, caring for my child, and shared experiences with other mothers, the things I may read, some of the values that I have regarding family. Identity is comprised of the ways we know ourselves. I am a spouse, mother, daughter, writer, speaker, coach, clinician, sibling, aunt, racquetball player and athlete. I am from a very rural area of upstate New York and now live in Massachusetts. These are the outer roles and activities that make up identity. There are other ways we form our identity as well including things such as our spiritual or religious beliefs, our political affiliation and views, our social class and education level all go into this complex web that we call our personal identity.

When you move to a new town or city, part of the adaptation is learning where things are and what services you want to access: where do you shop, get your car fixed, what health club suits your style, what church or temple congregation feels most welcoming and so on. Then there is the identity shift of being a resident in a new location. I lived in Marlborough, Massachusetts for about the past 20 years until about a year ago when I moved 35 miles east to Lexington. In the months following the move, whenever I would be asked, "Where are you from?" I would reply, "Marlborough, but I just moved to Lexington." After about a year, going through all of the phases of the transition and reaching resolution, I was able to drop the first half of my reply and simply state that I was from Lexington. But in the adaptation phase, I was still identified with my former city where I had lived for so many years.

The adaptation phase feels like a new pair of shoes – a little stiff and uncertain. It takes time to grow into and adapt to the change and the transition that follows. In adaptation you learn to live with the changes. You work with the doctors or rehab team who are helping your recovery rather than resist them and give up.

My adaptation after leaving employment for self-employment took quite a while. I had started a new business as a speaker and trainer as I was leaving my job (one of my anticipation activities). But in the emotional upheaval of losing my workplace, my identity as a social worker and the security of a weekly paycheck, I was not able to focus on the business and give it the attention it needed to grow. So having gone through nearly all of my savings, I refocused my efforts on my private counseling practice, which I maintained for a few years prior to leaving my job and which was aligned with my social work identity. I was still self-employed, but rather than leaving my job AND my profession all at once, I stepped back the degree of change during my adaptation phase. I built my private practice substantially and maintained that for another ten years before once again making the transition to be a full-time speaker, trainer and coach. This time, having a long history of experience with self-employment, I was able to focus, make the shift, and succeed. The change process often means re-navigating the waters when they become too rough to bear. Sometimes charting a new course takes longer, but offers greater security and comfort along the way.

4. Integration

The transition from adaptation to integration brings welcome relief because the acute phase of the transition is behind. In the integration phase, the new skills needed to live comfortably have been developed. For example, the physical rehabilitation has been successful for someone who has faced illness or injury. The person who has relocated to a new area has found the service providers and community organizations where they feel a sense of belonging and where there needs are being met. The new job is no longer mystifying as you move through the day once you learn your colleagues' names, what is expected of you, the office layout, and where to grab a good lunch. There is an emerging identity that is grounded in what was previously "the new." There is still some sense of connection to the old, but the new has now been embraced for what it is – the way life is at this phase. The shoes are still new and shiny, but they are broken in and molded to your feet in a way that brings a sense of comfort rather than distress.

5. Resolution

Once the adaptation has occurred, resolution follows closely behind. The resolution of a transition is the establishment of a new normal. The new is fully embraced and incorporated into your identity so that it becomes the new foundation for your life. The old is not forgotten or let go, rather it becomes an integral component of your life story. The resolution of a transition does not mean that you "get over it" but that you fully integrate each part of your history and life story, weaving a rich, textured tapestry. Life and its many transitions becomes a work of art that, at its best, is intentionally designed and created.

The table below summarizes the main phases of transition, along with the positive and difficult characteristics common to each phase.

Table 2. Transition Phases and Common Characteristics

Phase of Transition	Common Positive Characteristics of the Phase	Common Difficult Characteristics of the Phase
Anticipation	• Excitement • Feeling a sense of possibility • Feeling of personal power • Sense of optimism that the change will be for the better	• Uncertainty • Stress • Anxiety • Overwhelm • Dread
Change event	• New opportunity • Enhancement to the quality of life • Excitement • Enhanced energy	• Loss of function or capacity • Problems to be solved • Overwhelm • Shock • Stress
Adaptation	• Heightened learning • Bolstering social supports • Developing new skills • Developing new relationships	• Loss of identity • Sadness • Feeling "lost" or lack of direction • Feeling "ungrounded" • Uncertainty • Fear

		<ul><li>Overwhelm</li><li>Anger</li><li>Frustration</li></ul>
Integration	<ul><li>New confidence</li><li>Comfort and relief</li><li>Acceptance</li><li>New skills enhanced</li><li>New identity emerged</li><li>New optimism about the future emerged</li></ul>	<ul><li>Nostalgia for the old</li></ul>
Resolution	<ul><li>New skills mastered</li><li>New identity firmly in place</li><li>Sense of wholeness</li><li>A "new normal" is established</li></ul>	<ul><li>Boredom</li></ul>

Chapter Two: Understanding Your Change Temperament

A. Knowing Your Change Temperament

I entered motherhood when I was 42 years old. I was ripe with anticipation as I waited for my son to come home from his foster care placement in Guatemala. I had longed for the day I would begin a family of my own. The anticipation of getting the call that my embassy appointment date had been set was chilling and unnerving. I had visited my son 4 times over the 7 months since we were matched, and with each visit it became increasingly more grueling to leave behind my little guy.

I had stopped making plans for anything big as the anticipation of my flight to Guatemala and into motherhood loomed near. It was summertime, so invitations were plentiful for weekend getaways, family reunions and weddings. My repeated reply was, "I can't make any plans now. I'll be off to get my son and will want to be settling in."

The call finally did come after what seemed like a lifetime of waiting and anticipation (I know that sounds a bit dramatic, but ask any adoptive mother and you will hear the same sentiment!). I flew to Guatemala City on August 1st to take my son for the last time, this time forever. We would make it official on August 4th, 2006 as we finalized the adoption at the Guatemala Embassy and then flew home the next day to begin our lives together. True joy, unabated bliss… If it weren't for that little thing called *The Transition.*

Any new mother will tell you how having a first child is a roller coaster of emotion from the highest of highs to the occasional desperate moments of fatigue, worry and overwhelm. The sleepless nights, the uncertainty of each sound, learning the ways of your newborn, it all takes its toll. But I hadn't just become a new mother, I had become a new mother at 42 years of age – and my child was a toddler! Good Lord, what was I thinking? The transition to motherhood was desperately difficult, more than I ever could have imagined. My son was an Easy Baby. I mean that in the grandest sense. He was a front-runner in a unique category of children that few lucky mothers have the blessing to enjoy. He always slept well, ate well, had an easy-going temperament and aside from recurrent ear infections, was almost never sick. Even when he was up at night with ear infections, I remember pacing the floors while he merely cuddled into my chest and laid in the comfort of my arms. No middle of the night screaming, no skyrocketing fevers, he was just too sick to sleep and wanted to be held.

Given my immense excitement, planning and anticipation of becoming a mother coupled with having the easiest baby on the planet, you would think the road into motherhood would have been an easy ride. Yes, it would be reasonable to think so. But then there's me and my temperament for change.

In my excited, optimistic anticipation, I had completely underestimated the impact of having to care for a baby. This challenge included not only the practical changes like feeding, tending, loving, soothing and keeping him from killing himself on an hourly basis by hurling himself head-long down a flight of stairs or other similar antics – but the emotional changes of the loss of independence, the ease of taking my morning shower, the ability to finish a sentence with my spouse without being interrupted. Every experienced parent tells every expectant parent, "You have no idea what you are getting into." I knew that was true. I even told people "I don't know what I don't know about becoming a mother. "

Having been fairly adventurous in my career – making lots of changes and rolling with the flow relatively well – I had assumed that I tolerated change and would similarly sail into the transition of motherhood with some sort of grace and ease. What I did not recognize was that my change temperament regarding my career, where I am fluid, confident and creative, was strong and stable. My change temperament for my lifestyle with regard to my freedom, planning and independence, was drastically more marginal. Prior to becoming a mother, I had no clue!

So what is a *change temperament* and why is it important to recognize yours? Change temperaments are your response capacity to change and transition. By *response capacity*, I mean how well you "roll" with life versus to what degree life's twists and turns tie you up in knots and cause some difficulty for you.

Over the years as a therapist and professional coach, I have come to identify four different change temperaments. They are:

1. Change averse
2. Change sensitive
3. Change neutral
4. Change seeker

Before we go into each of these temperaments, it is important to recognize a few things about change temperaments in general.

First, change temperaments are not necessarily consistent over time or over various life areas. Just as there are developmental milestones in one's personality development, relationship development and brain development, I have come to see that change temperament has a developmental cycle as well. Typically, change temperaments are "low" or more fragile in the early and later years of the life span and "high" or strong in the young adult and adult years. Young children thrive on consistency, stability and predictability. As a social worker, when I see a child having behavioral difficulty in school, one of the many factors I assess relates to any significant changes in the home or school setting. Children are incredibly sensitive to change – it makes their world feel unpredictable and hence, unsafe.

At the other end of the life spectrum, elderly people also need a great deal of stability, consistency and predictability in their daily lives. Disruptions in routine, changes in living arrangements and loss of friends and loved ones are often significant challenges for the elderly for very similar reasons as with young children. Change represents a feeling of lack of safety and the elderly are in many ways vulnerable like young children.

At both ends of the life spectrum, whether with children or with elders, there are many changes happening in one's physical body and capacities, one's social setting, and one's outer structure. Children are adapting to the social and educational environment of school, while elders are adapting to the change in identity at the relinquishment of one's career and the transition in the relationships around work, as well as the change in social status of going from the ranks for the employed to those of the retired. It seems to take all of the psychological strength of the individual to go through those changes, leaving little energy available to roll with changes in day-to-day living. All change represents loss and uncertainty and particularly in the early and later phases of life, when people are at their most vulnerable, loss and uncertainty are harder to bear.

It is almost as if there is a bell curve in relation to change tolerance. At the earlier and later years of the life span, there is lower change tolerance, whereas in the early-mid, mid, and late-midlife years there is greater resilience for change. See Figure 1.

Figure 1. Change Tolerance Curve

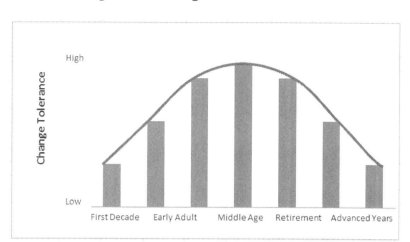

Second, change temperaments can vary over different areas of life. As I mentioned above, I generally had greater ease with changes in my career than I did with the change in becoming a mother. Career transitions generally impact one life area, although there can be lesser residual effects into other areas as well. For example, if a career change leads to a significant pay raise that would impact one's lifestyle, financial goals, ability to travel and greater economic freedom. Becoming a parent, having a major medical challenge or crisis, an accident that leaves you incapacitated in some way – these are changes that penetrate into the very fiber of the way we live.

I had a good friend named Pete who was in a car accident that resulted in his becoming quadriplegic. Pete was a strong, social and outgoing man, successful in his career and in his social life. The accident impacted every aspect of his life from the moment it occurred: his job, his identity, how he was perceived by others, his social relationships, what he needed to learn in order to be fully independent again, his physical capacity and limitations, his financial situation – truly every area of his life was impacted by the change from going from able-bodied to wheelchair-bound.

The *change* occurred the moment he had the accident, but the *transition* in Pete's life lasted for several years beyond.

Generally, the bigger the change and the more life areas that are impacted, the greater impact on one's psychic, emotional and relational world. In other words, greater change equals greater impact. Still, there are enormous variations in how people respond to even the greatest life changes. These variations depend on one's overall change temperament.

Below is a look at the major change temperaments:

1. Change Averse

People who are change averse seek to maintain their outer world in the same fashion and manner as much as possible. They are not prone to big, adventurous travel or moving across the country for the next, exciting new job. In fact, they may not explore changing jobs at all. They are the type of people who would stay married, even unhappily, rather than pursue a different relationship. I traveled to a beautiful Caribbean island of Bimini in 2004. Bimini is an incredibly small island – just a quarter mile wide and approximately 4 miles long. You can easily tour the whole island in a day – several times! I met a man there who really intrigued me due to his distinct change averse temperament. Francis was a 78-year-old man who was born and raised on the tiny island. In conversing with him, I learned that he had never lived anywhere other than this quarter mile by four-mile stretch of land in the middle of the Caribbean. Given that there is frequent air traffic off the island that goes to the Bahamas or Miami (via a pontoon plane that lands in Bimini Bay), I assumed he often traveled to the US or Grand Bahama Island. But when I spoke with Francis, he informed me that he had not left the island for over 35 years. The last time he left was to attend his brother's memorial service in Miami, and then he immediately returned to Bimini. I was shocked and intrigued by this lovely man's demeanor as he described his experience. He was quite content with his island life. I can imagine he knew that island like the back of his hand, able to walk every private path that had gotten etched in the sand by the locals or the schoolchildren. I felt an odd mix of pity and envy for the old man. Pity because it is such a big world out there and for how much Francis will never see, and envy that he was completely content with his four and a quarter miles of this planet.

Francis is someone I would describe as change averse. He not only sought out no change, he structured his life to remain the same as possible year in and year out. As you can see in Francis' life story, being change averse is not necessarily a detriment. You can still lead a happy, contended life – so long as the winds of change are not thrust upon you.

2. Change Sensitive

My Uncle Mike is someone who strikes me as being change sensitive. He has lived on the same farmhouse his entire life. His farmhouse is adorned with many of the same furnishings that his great grandparents purchased; lovely, large ornate antiques fill the living room and throughout the house. He has worked as a high school science teacher for his entire adult life. He has been married to the same woman, spending time with the same friends, canoeing the same river, wearing the same type of clothes, with the same haircut for as long as I can remember. I love him for that. There is something extremely comforting about being around Uncle Mike. He is the picture of stability. Our family vacations at the farm are predictable and yet oh so memorable. From this description, you might think that Uncle Mike is change averse rather than change sensitive. I see the difference as being that he has sought to change his teaching job twice in thirty or so years. People who are change averse quite literally never seek change. Uncle Mike also travels from time to time, when family commitments call him away from the farm. He is a steady man, as solid as the earth beneath the farm upon which he was raised, and where he will most likely also die.

3. Change Neutral

Change neutral people neither seek nor avoid change. They have the emotional capacity for tolerating transitions, yet do not crave the energy and excitement that transitions often bring. A client of mine, let's call him Frank, is someone who I would describe as change neutral. In his earlier years, just out of college, Frank lived in 5 different countries over the course of 7 years. He loved traveling, taking in new cultures, learning new languages, taking on jobs that were in the service sector of international education. Frank chose to marry soon out of graduate school, took a job with a company that was fully in line with his values, and settled down into a comfortable suburban lifestyle with a spouse and children. He occasionally speaks of his desire to pick up and move to another country, pursing life as an ex-patriot, and yet, he has developed a comfortable ease with coaching youth soccer, going to parent-teacher meetings and volunteering in his community. There is nothing about him that would lead you to believe that in his twenties he was traveling the world full of adventure, and yet there is also nothing about him that says if the right opportunity presented itself tomorrow that he would be unable to mobilize his resources and family and make a big shift into the unknown. Being change neutral is an advantageous position of being able to embrace the charge of transition or the comfort of stability equally well.

4. Change Seeker

Change seekers are those who not only embrace change, they seek and initiate it – the more frequently the better. Change seekers generally make better entrepreneurs than employees, are often excellent idea-people, but not great at follow through and are fed by near-constant stimulation of new and different people, circumstances and challenges. I am sure you have a friend or relative who is a change seeker – or maybe some of you are as well – those who often receive the question, "So what is it that you are up to now?"

My friend, Maurice, is a change seeker through and through. He has made (and lost) millions of dollars in numerous different ventures in wildly divergent fields over the 20 or so years that I have known him. While he has been married to the same woman for over 30 years, he also managed to start another family in another part of the country and keep it all underground for many years. He constantly renovates his home. While Maurice may be an extreme example, you can see the repeated pattern of seeking new stimuli and change. People who are change seekers fall into this spectrum. They thrive on what is new and often quickly grow bored with what has been mastered or accomplished. They are "start-up" people, quite unlike those who are steady and consistent like my Uncle Mike or Francis from Bimini.

In a later chapter, we will look at what things you can do to help you manage the sea of emotions that often accompany life transitions. For now, let's get more specific regarding understanding and identifying your general change temperament. The following inventory is designed to help you look more closely at how you have responded to life changes so that you are better equipped to face the transitions looming ahead.

Exercise: Identify Your Change Temperament

Please rate your perception of yourself in relation to the comments below on a scale of 0-5 with zero indicating "Never/Rarely" and five indicating "Always/Most Often."

_____ I tend to get somewhat anxious or irritable when things do not go as I thought they would.

_____ I have stayed at the same place of employment for more than 5-10 years.

_____ I have tried to make some changes in my life, but am often not able to follow through (i.e. weight loss, exercise routine, dietary change or other type of self-improvement).

_____ I have had difficulty "letting go" of the past or getting over some life changes (i.e. an old romance, my childhood home, college life, etc.).

_____ I have experienced periods of anxiety or depression before, during or after some life change.

_____ I have lived in the same geographic location for the past 10 or more years.

_____ I keep relatively the same hair and clothing style without wide variation in my physical appearance.

_____ Other people have sometimes told me I need to "get over it" and move on from some past situation or circumstance.

_____ I hesitate to volunteer for new assignments at work, even if I am fully prepared for them.

_____ I am reluctant begin new adventures or pursue new opportunities.

_____ I have a lot of ideas, but often do not put them into action.

_____ I get anxious when new opportunities emerge and hesitate to take action on them.

_____ I generally avoid or resist traveling to new places.

_____ I get worn out when I start a new venture, travel to an unfamiliar place or begin a new job.

_____ I rarely make changes to my home environment.

_____ Total

Scoring:

0-18 = Change Seeker

19-37 = Change Neutral

38-55 = Change Sensitive

56-75 = Change Averse

B. Why Know Your Change Temperament?

Now that we have looked at the four variations of how people approach change, let's talk about why it matters. What difference does it make to recognize and develop an awareness of your personal change temperament and perhaps the temperaments others?

All effective change begins with awareness. To develop a solid, usable change-management and transition strategy, you first must understand your common reactions to life transitions and then establish a course to address your unique needs. You can only change or address that which you can see. Developing a keen awareness of your change temperament allows you to establish the right amount and type of support that you need to assist the transition you are facing and make it go as smoothly as possible.

When I entered motherhood, I greatly underestimated my change temperament, and it cost me dearly. I was unprepared for how significantly I would be impacted by the change of having a child. It was not entirely a naïve oversight. In the anticipation phase of my transition to motherhood, I was focused on the positive aspects of this important life change. And yet, had I looked more deeply at my change temperament, I would have garnered the support I needed to get through the first year or so of transition with greater ease and less stress.

Those like me who are more sensitive or even averse to change need to incorporate this awareness into any planned transition process. Similarly, when an unexpected life change occurs, knowing that one has a sensitive change temperament will provide guidance to seek greater support to minimize or eliminate other life changes while going through the unexpected transition.

In the last chapter of this book, we will explore specific tools and strategies that help people navigate the inevitable seas of change.

For now, you have taken an important first step in assessing your own change temperament and beginning to think about what challenges may emerge as you enter into coming life transitions.

Chapter Three: The Problem with Change

I live outside of Boston, Massachusetts, a city rich with American history. I have visited Plymouth Plantation where the pilgrims are said to have landed. I have enjoyed the reenactment on the Lexington Battle Green, said to be the birthplace of the American Revolution. My old office in central Massachusetts was one of the oldest buildings in the town, circa 1799. Historic buildings; narrow, cobblestone streets; the certainty and permanence of the Atlantic Ocean nearby – all of these icons of stability, so remarkably unchanged.

I have seen images on the internet and in a magazine publication recently of a McDonald's Happy Meal that was purchased and left sitting untouched for several years. It was seemingly unchanged. No mold, nothing falling apart, nothing rotted away. Similarly a science teacher, Mr. Roger Bennatti from Blue Hill, Maine did an experiment with a group of students to examine the impact of food preservatives on the life of a Twinkie. That experiment was conducted 31 years ago, and up until this year, the Twinkie sat *fully intact* in Mr. Bennatti's classroom. Thirty-one years! It had grown hard and dry and lost some of its original color, but otherwise looked quite similar to one you might have purchased in a store today (although I hear that they have gone out of production! Wonder if it had anything to do with Mr. Bennatti's "experiment!"). Such drastic lack of change in our food is less than comforting!

Think of how many changes your life and your body have endured in the past 31 years. Really, think about it. Where were you 31 years ago? What stage of life were you in? Were you even born yet!? Thirty-one years ago I was … Oh, never mind. Let's just say it was a *much* different time in my life. And look at our lives relative to the cobblestone streets and brownstones in downtown Boston, or better yet, our lives in relation to the majesty of the oceans, the mountains, the Redwoods. We are a blip on the screen of the Universe.

It is an odd feeling to think that rocks, buildings and maybe even Twinkies will outlive us. While the "shelf life" of a human being has grown considerably, it still is dwarfed by the seeming eternity of the natural world. Our lives are so small in comparison. Nature goes on and on, and yet we often struggle over the day-to-day changes that come our way and those we intentionally implement (or try to) in our lives.

One of the blessings of living in New England is the artful display nature brings with the passing of each season. It is spring now, and in what seemed like a mere blink, the trees intuitively knew how to blossom into a sea of whites, reds and pinks. Then again without as much as one instruction or the need for a strategic plan, the trees all turned shades of green, lining our streets and yards with rich beauty. They will provide us with shade and breezes over the hot summer months, and then again, without anyone establishing a plan of action, these same trees will burst into a pinwheel of color with red, orange, yellow and rust covering our landscapes before falling to create a barren and beautiful landscape ready for the winter snows.

We should be so lucky! Can you imagine undergoing such drastic change every few months? If you struggle at all with making change (and who doesn't?), you would probably need a good dose of anxiety medication and a therapist to tolerate that much change every year. Why is that? What is it about facing life change that often creates such disequilibrium to our inner world? Why are we, as human beings, so much less adaptable than nature around us?

The challenge of writing a brief primer on life transition and change is that there are so many different kinds of transitions that come to us in such varied ways and impact us quite differently across our life span. Planned versus unplanned change exist in very different contexts. The primary difference is that planned change exists in the context of choice whereas unplanned change most often does not include having directed the transition that occurred. Planned changes such as a wedding, retirement, graduation, new job or relocation, establishing a new goal or set of goals occur because we have given our assent to these events; we have engaged in a series of decisions, actions and behaviors that resulted in the change. That volitional choice and those decisions, actions and behaviors form the context inside of which the change takes place.

Unplanned change, on the other hand, most often exists in a context of needing to respond to an external circumstance that one has not chosen, designed and implemented. A car accident, illness, eviction or a breakup most often just land on our lap, often with no notice. The context is entirely different.

A. Choice and Change

Generally, the greater the degree of choice regarding a change, and the greater the pleasure the change brings, the less difficulty one will have adapting to the change. Conversely, the less choice one has regarding the change and the greater the discord it brings, the more difficulty one will likely have adapting to and resolving this sort of change. For example, I have wanted to own a home on the St. Lawrence River in upstate New York since I graduated from high school and left the area. The St. Lawrence is a majestic river, and is the northern border between Canada and the United States. It is decorated with over 1200 islands (and thus is known as the Thousand Islands region) and is the seaway for ocean-going ships traveling between the Great Lakes and the Atlantic Ocean. It is idyllic and I have loved it since I was a child. My cousin knew that I wanted to purchase his mother's cottage from him someday, and I hoped that my dream would one day come true. My "one day" came much sooner than I anticipated when my cousin told me he was ready to sell the cottage four years ago and I was met with a choice – either fulfill a dream at a time that I was not financially prepared to do so, or lose the opportunity. This is the kind of change that often causes stress in our lives – the change of a welcomed opportunity that also requires a good degree of risk, requiring faith and courage to move forward.

Purchasing a summer home was a life change for which I was not yet financially prepared, which could cause stress, leading to a missed opportunity. It was also a life change over which I had total control – I could decide to purchase it or not. Given the degree of pleasure I felt at fulfilling this dream, and the anticipation of raising my son on the St. Lawrence River, I was able to adapt to the unplanned change quite easily and make the decision to purchase the cottage; an adaptation that occurred quickly and one that I will enjoy for the rest of my life!

Of course, one never knows if taking such a risk will lead to years of happy memories or financial ruin, if a bad breakup will lead to years of despair or to the meeting of one's true love, or if the exciting new job will result in smashing career success or being fired by the boss from hell. We are all met with these choices and changes in life, and short of having a wise and predicting crystal ball, we cannot foresee the long-range impact on either a planned or unplanned change.

There is a Zen Buddhist story of a farmer who had diligently worked his crops for many years. One day his horse ran away. Upon hearing the news, his neighbors came to visit. "Such bad luck," they said sympathetically.

"Maybe," the farmer replied. The next morning the horse returned, bringing with it three other wild horses. "How wonderful," the neighbors exclaimed.

"Maybe," replied the old man. The following day, his son tried to ride one of the untamed horses, was thrown, and broke his leg. The same neighbors came to call on the farmer to express their sympathy of his son's seeming misfortune. "Maybe," answered the farmer.

The day after the son broke his leg, military officials came to the village to take away the young men into the army. Seeing that the son's leg was broken, they passed him by, letting him remain with his father. The neighbors congratulated the farmer on how well things had turned out. "Maybe," said the farmer.

This simple story reflects the truth of life transition and change. We truly never know the ultimate destiny after any given circumstance. We would be prudent to borrow the wisdom of the farmer, keeping our hearts and minds open during change with a simple expression of "maybe."

B. Why Is It So Hard to Change?

I have heard this question a thousand times as a coach and therapist over the past 25 years. Why is it so hard to change our behavior and emotions? You all know family members or co-workers who are steadfastly going to resist any new idea or direction in the family or the company. Perhaps you are one of the loud protestors of change. What is it that makes it so incredibly hard to make even the simplest of changes?

As a therapist over the years, I have counseled people who deal with anxiety, helping them begin using mindfulness meditation as part of their active treatment. I have worked with people for week after week, trying to get them to simply sit down for a brief five minutes to count their breath. That's it. Just sit still for five minutes and count the breath. I can honestly say that not once, not one single person ever did the assignment in the first week (or often several weeks) after hearing the recommendation. I would offer all sorts of facts and scholarly articles pointing to the benefits of meditation in the treatment of anxiety – still, nothing. No change. All sorts of reasons and rationalizations would emerge in sessions following the instruction on mindfulness, until finally each individual would admit, it is just really hard to change, even when it is clearly change for the better.

There is a funny Bob Newhart clip on You Tube in which Newhart is playing a therapist seeing an anxious and troubled-looking young woman. For each concern that she raises, from claustrophobia to bulimia to self-destructive relationships with men – Newhart responds with a quick and assertive, "Stop it!" Oh, if only it were so easy! We so often know what to do, and yet, over and over again, we fail to do what we know. I have often told my coaching clients that if I did nothing more than hold them accountable for doing what they said they would do, they would get more than their money's worth in value. And so far every single one of them agrees!

Even the apostle Paul lamented in the New Testament Letter to the Romans[1], "I do not understand what I do. For what I want to do I do not do, but what I hate I do." It seems to be an age-old dilemma that our will and our human nature are at odds with one another. Our will wants to do the right thing, and yet our human nature pulls at us to be lazy, just get by, and make all manner of excuses for behavior of which we do not approve.

You have heard the expression that we are creatures of habit, but what exactly does this mean? How are habits formed and how do we undo them to create new ones that are better for our growth and our lives?

---

1. New American Bible - Romans 7:15

C. The Neurology of Change

We are fortunate to live in a time when contemporary neuroscience has taught us much about the workings of the brain, and we understand so much more about behavior and change now than we ever have before.

Some behavior change experts assert that there are only two things that motivate change in human beings: avoiding pain or seeking pleasure. These specialists believe that these are the two reasons we initiate changes in our habits, behaviors and ways of being. The basis of all change first begins with awareness of an area of discomfort. It is either discomfort with a current situation or the discomfort of wanting something greater. This awareness gives rise, sooner or later, to the thought that a change is needed.

This approach is far too reductionist for my liking. I believe there is a tertiary motivation for change, one that wells up from deep within our being and perhaps has its roots in our very soul. That third motivation is desire. Not the clinging, driven, jealous sort of desire that we are spoon-fed by media, but the sort of desire that gives rise to our very being. The sort of desire I am referring to requires patience to find full expression in your life. Like a mighty ship sailing on an endless sea seeking its final port and safety before mooring firm and coming to rest. The sort of desire I am speaking of is the deepest desires of your heart. For some it is to find a great love, for others it is to offer a great service to the world, for still others it is to reach excellence in their chosen field. But far too often, we give up on our dreams, leaving that One Great Desire buried deep within the sea of our soul.

To understand how these three motivations for change impact us, however, we first must understand the way the brain operates with regard to that behavior, motivation and change. When we do a thing over and over again, it creates a pathway in our brain. The more the brain "practices" that pathway through repetition of a certain behavior, the harder it is to undo that pathway to create a new one. The repeated behavior becomes easier and easier over time – often even occurring below our level of conscious awareness. We know that young children need much more sleep than adults need. One of the main reasons for this is that children are in the process of forming new neuropathways while we, as adults, have millions of them already established[2]. I'm sure you have heard someone who has tried to quit smoking, struggling not only with the withdrawals of the chemical addiction, but also the behavioral habits of having a morning cigarette with their cup of coffee, or that they always smoke in the car, or some other associative behavior that they have with the smoking. That reflexive behavioral pattern is due to established neuropathways.

We have neuropathways for everything. Our morning routine is a neuropathway. My client, David, has a morning routine of getting up, getting a cup of coffee and immediately going to his computer to check email and read the news. For weeks he lamented that he wanted to get more exercise, but insisted he had no extra time to fit it in. I asked him to describe his typical day (because it is very rare that difficulty with change is really about lack of time). As he walked me through his day, I saw several pockets where he could get some exercise, starting with his morning routine. Yet when I suggested that he replace his morning email checking, which is sedentary, with a morning walking, which would accomplish his goal, David resisted fiercely.

Trying to get him up and take a morning walk instead of sitting at the computer is like trying to get him up and jump out the window! Even though he clearly knew he wanted to get more exercise, and he could see that he could easily replace checking email and reading the news with going for the walk, changing the behavior from the email checking to the walking was too big of a

---

2.   (http://health.usnews.com/health-news/family-health/sleep/articles/2007/09/06/kids-and-sleep-they-need-more)

leap.

The will says, "Go for the walk, you fool! You're not getting any younger and those extra 10 pounds don't look good on you!" To which the brain's patterned neuropathway responds by walking directly to the coffee pot and then the computer. The brain automatically does what is familiar. It requires far less energy to engage in a behavior that already has a neuropathway well established.

The longer that one has been engaged with a relationship, activity or place, the harder it is to lose it via a life transition. It is much easier to move on from a job that you occupied for 6 months than where you have devoted your entire career. It is easier to leave a city after a few years, than to leave the only geographic location you have ever known. Most often, the longer the relationship we have with a person, place or thing, the greater the sense of loss. The reasons for this may seem obvious on the surface, we grow to love the people and places we have known, they bring us pleasure and comfort. This is true, but there is a greater reason that lies in the confines of the organ of our brain.

The longer you do anything, the more you pattern your brain to expect it to be that way. You develop a predictive sense of the world that makes life easier. Your brain literally develops neuropathways so that you "don't have to think." How many times have you arrived at a familiar destination such as your workplace or a good friend's home, only to realize that you have no recollection of driving there? Or when someone asks you the driving route to a place to which you often go, how many times have you said, "Oh, I could drive there with my eyes closed, but I can't think of each turn to tell you how to do it"? This is the type of brain patterning that takes place in every area of our lives. It is adaptive so that we can reserve our mental energy for more challenging tasks like problem solving, relationship negotiation and all of our creative work.

Think of it this way: If you have a well-worn path between your house and a neighbor's house on the other side of the woods, is it easier for you to walk the worn path or to blaze a new trail? Of course it is easier to walk the path. The same is true for your brain. It literally takes less energy for your brain to follow its old, predictable habits and routines than to blaze new trails of different behavior. So even when the change you want to institute is for your good, and clearly something you want to initiate, it takes energy to overcome the pre-programming in your neural network in your brain. You will notice that you become fatigued more easily, you may be irritable or even short-tempered. This is due to the fact that when you are in unfamiliar places, you are using a great deal more mental "fuel" to process things that you do literally without thinking in your familiar habitat. These are some of the symptoms associated with the neurology of behavior change.

All of this is not to say that we should stay stuck in our familiar surroundings, routines and relationships to avoid the mental and emotional challenge of new places. It is solely to point out that as we experience a loss of the familiar – either by plan or merely due to the winds of change – we need to know the impact of this loss on our overall functioning so that we can best adapt to the newness we are facing.

D. The Psychology of Change

To complicate things further, there is also a part of our personality that functions to keep things the same, to remain static and predictable. That part of our personality is called the *ego*. It is that "little voice in your head" that is often critical and cautious. Our ego mind constantly rationalizes and justifies our patterned behavior because it is familiar – and familiar means safety to the ego.

David adamantly wanted more exercise and yet, his ego mind says,

"Walk, schmalk! I can't start my day without knowing what's going on in the world! I'll just take a quick look and see what's happening." Self-talk such as this represents a process called *rationalization*, which is a psychological defense that helps to maintain homeostasis, or more simply said, lack of change. It is the part of your mind that gives you permission to do what you do not want to do (or conversely to NOT do something that you want to do such as David taking a morning walk). This process of rationalization, when used repeatedly over time is what psychotherapists call *cognitive distortions*. It is a way that we give ourselves permission to break the rules – our own rules and those imposed on us by others. It is what allows you to eat that big, luscious piece of cake while saying you want to lose ten pounds. You rationalize by saying something along the lines of, "I've had a hard day so I deserve a little treat." Or, "I will do it just this once. I've been good for the past few days." I'm sure you recognize this voice in your own head. The use of cognitive distortions is the process that allows for little indiscretions such as the piece of cake when trying to improve your diet, as well as much bigger challenges such as having that one more drink, and then another ("This will be the last one."), or fudging your expense report when you turn it into the office ("They should be paying me more anyway."). In fact, I once worked with incarcerated male sex offenders and it was this same process of cognitive distortion that allowed these men to engage in egregious and illegal behavior, even when they knew it could ultimately hurt others and cause their demise. The PROCESS of employing cognitive distortions is the same, whether insignificant or life altering in effect. The degree to which we allow ourselves to employ this process depends on a myriad of other psychological factors that are well beyond the scope of this book. For our purposes here, it is important to recognize the degree to which you engage in your own cognitive distortions that allow the perpetuation of behaviors that you long to change. To help you begin identifying your own cognitive distortions (we all have them to some degree), here is a list of some very common ones that get in the way of creating lasting change:

Cognitive Distortions

I will only do this once.

This will be my last time.

No one will find out.

Nobody knows I do this.

I deserve to do this because ....   (fill in the blank, often things like I am lonely, I am tired, I have had a hard day).

I really cannot do any better than this because… (fill in the blank: I am not smart enough, I am lazy, I haven't had the advantages in life that others have had).

I will start tomorrow.

I need this to relax (often a harmful substance such as alcohol or marijuana, but also hours in front of video games or computer screens).

Just once won't hurt anything.

It is important to recognize that the use of cognitive distortions is not necessarily out of the realm of normal, as in being some form of psychopathology. The point here is to recognize the ways in which you say things to yourself that give you permission to avoid the change you want to initiate in your life. All change begins with awareness. You are aware of your desire for a change, but you also need to be aware of the shenanigans your ego can play in order to keep things the same.

While the context of life change that is planned and those that are cast upon us is vastly different, there are some common characteristics that occur. So in order to keep this book as a quick and easy primer on change, versus an encyclopedia on the topic, let's look at the common characteristics of the problem with change.

E. Common Characteristics of the Problem with Change

1. Change as a Loss of Identity

Having and maintaining a stable identity is crucial to our overall emotional well-being. By *identity* I mean how you know yourself.

This may sound a little silly or redundant. Maybe you are thinking, "What do you mean, 'How I know myself?' I just know myself!" While this is true, you know yourself in a particular context of meaning, roles and relationships that quite literally give rise to who you are. Remove yourself from this context, and you could, and in fact would, show up as a very different you. Let's say for example that you know yourself as being a married, professional, liberal, Democrat, straight, artistic female from the mid-west. All of these roles or identifications are part of what make you, you! You can quickly see that if you wave a magic wand and were suddenly cast into a life of a swinging single, working class, conservative, Republican, gay, athletically-inclined male from New York City you would have wildly different experience of being you! What makes you the unique individual that you have become are the roles, values and relationships through which you define yourself. Your identity includes all of the things mentioned here and more.

Table 3. Identifying Characteristics

Components of Identity
Social class and economic power
Social, ethical and spiritual values (liberal, conservative, traditional, contemporary)
Professional affiliation and employment (tradesman, business owner, professional, etc.)
Political affiliation (liberal, conservative, libertarian, moderate)
Hobbies (sports, arts, entertainment)
Marital and familial status (wife, mother, daughter, sibling, etc.)
Gender identity (male, female, transgender, girly girl, tomboy, man's man)
Race and ethnicity
Physical abilities and stature
Sexual identity (gay, straight, bisexual)
Education level
Geographic location (rural, urban, suburban, southern, northeast, and so on)
Language (your primary language as well as other language affiliations you have)

You will notice that many of your friends and colleagues share many of the same identifying characteristics as you. That is because when we surround ourselves with "people like us" we see our self and our identity mirrored back to us and in a sense, this helps us to feel that we are okay. The more we can look outside ourselves and see people like us, the more we feel safe, secure and validated. Look around at our world – in gross generalities in our country, the Northeast and west coast are liberal, the south is conservative. Cities are generally more progressive than rural areas, and people of similar ethnicities gather together in geographic strongholds (i.e. Chinatown, Little Italy, and so on).

When you lose any one of these pieces of your identity, you experience some degree of emotional turmoil until there is some resolution of the lost identity. I was a therapist during the beginning of the sexual abuse scandal and crisis in the Catholic Church in 2002. During that time I saw numerous therapy clients who were experiencing psychological distress, not only due to the catastrophic nature of the allegations being raised, but also due to the depth of which each individual's core identity as a Catholic was being shaken.

When we experience life transition and change, there is always a loss of identity. When you get married, you lose the identity as a single person; when you retire, you lose the identity of your workplace or your business; when you are widowed, you lose the identity as someone who is married. These are significant changes to how you have known yourself in the world. My mother, twice widowed, often complains of feeling like she's the "third wheel" and often avoids socializing with friends she has known for 30 or 40 years because she no longer has the identity of being married.
I am certain that her friends are not thinking, "Oh, we had better not have Norma along since she doesn't have her husband any longer." It is in my mother's self-perception that there has been a change in her status, how she knows herself socially and in this thing called her *social identity*.

2. Change as a Loss of the Familiar

Perhaps the most global and challenging aspect of any life transition is simply yet profoundly the loss of what once was, the loss of what was familiar and known. Let's face it, we are creatures of habit. We thrive on consistency, predictability and stasis. It requires much more energy and attention to live life when constantly presented with new things to which you need to adapt. Take the simple chore of grocery shopping and imagine what that would be like at your local grocery store versus how it would feel and what energy and attention it would require if you were grocery shopping in a foreign country, or even simply when your familiar grocery store has been renovated and items have been rearranged. When you have moved from one location to another – perhaps across town or around the globe, you know the feeling of being disoriented when you need to sort out the simplest tasks of daily living.

Familiar routines, places and relationships ground us. That is, the familiar gives us a solid place to stand in life, and from that grounded place, we are able to live more fully. I'm sure you have all heard the expression, or perhaps used it yourself, "I've lost my grounding." What that means is that what we once relied on for stability, comfort and predictability has been shaken or removed.

When our sense of grounding and our identity is entirely based on external factors, we are more vulnerable to the winds of change. People die, relationships end, jobs come and go, companies close. This is one of the reasons why it is so crucial to develop a strong sense of inner identity and purpose that includes but supersedes the external conditions and relationships in our lives. Our inner identity consists of our values, the meaning we give to our lives, our vision for how we want our lives to be and our sense of personal mission or purpose; i.e. what we say our life is for and about. When you develop a strong sense of purpose, you immediately have an inner compass that helps to guide you toward the expression of your purpose, desires and your personal values.

The American novelist and playwright, James Baldwin addresses this beautifully in his eloquent quote:

> *"Any real change implies the breakup of the world as one has always known it, the loss of all that gave one an identity, the end of safety. And at such a moment, unable to see and not daring to imagine what the future will now bring forth, one clings to what one knew, or thought one knew; to what one possessed or dreamed that he possessed. Yet, it is only when man (sic) is able, without bitterness or self-pity, to surrender a dream he has long cherished or a privilege he has long possessed that he is set free — he has set himself free — for higher dreams, for greater privileges."* [3]

3. Change as Loss of Self-Esteem

Losing something that feels like it is a part of you can quite literally feel like a part of you has died. This sense of losing a part of one's self often leads to at least a temporary loss of self-esteem. This is particularly true when the loss is something that is very central to one's identity such as a career or family relationship. In fact, one study done by the Shell Corporation over the years 1973 to 2003 found that people who retire at 55 are 89% more likely to die in the 10 years after retirement than those who retire at 65. This is an astounding statistic. This difference could not be attributed to the effects of sex, socioeconomic status, or calendar year of the study. This study points to the significant impact of the loss of identity, self-esteem and status through one's career and profession. It also speaks volumes of the importance of developing a strong sense of inner identity and purpose as a means to bolster self-esteem, rather than relying solely on external validation, support and connection to feed our healthy sense of self.

---

3. ("Faulkner and Desegregation" in *Partisan Review* (Fall 1956); republished in *Nobody Knows My Name: More Notes of a Native Son* (1961)).

Maintaining a healthy self-esteem is critical for our successful journeying through the stages of life. By *self-esteem*, I mean your sense of valuing yourself, feeling good about who you are in the world, your gifts, talents, contributions and the life you are creating. Self-esteem is integral to overall happiness and sense of life satisfaction. It is essentially being at peace with who you are and are not. Some may wonder which comes first – is it that external conditions lead to self-esteem or is it that one has a strong sense of self-esteem, and that leads to creating a satisfying life? When I look at this question, I look at all the incredibly talented, world-renowned performers and athletes who seemingly crashed and burned despite having talent, fame, wealth and the adoration of fans. Which comes first? I think loving the self comes first, which then creates a life in which happiness and fulfillment emerge.

When your sense of self-esteem is tied to an external condition – whether raising children or running a successful business – you are much more vulnerable to a loss of self-esteem when the external condition is gone.

I was hired by Max, a 60-year-old successful businessman, for just this reason. Fortunately, Max had the foresight to recognize what a tremendous loss he would face should he decide to sell his multiple businesses and retire so he decided to hire a coach well before he faced that life change. He wanted to ensure that he was well prepared with a new lifestyle and an identity that was broader than what he had cultivated over his 35 years in business. After a few years of deepening and broadening his identity to include being an avid world traveler, sailor, outdoor sports enthusiast, a volunteer on some local community boards and his church, and scaling back his overall involvement in his business, he saw that he had created such a rich and fulfilling life that retirement was less compelling overall. He enjoyed owning his businesses, which mostly ran independently with the right people in the right positions, and yet he still had a connection to something larger, as well as the enjoyment of the ongoing income his businesses provided. He also did a great deal of introspective work in discerning his core values in life, and began exploring his connection to spirituality through greater participation in his church, meditation and other personal development classes. Max was able to cultivate a sense of self-esteem through a deep inner connection, giving back to the community, engaging in humanitarian mission trips and expanding his skills as an athlete rather than just from his identity as a business owner.

4. Change as Something to Fear

Fear of change is probably the most prevalent reason that people resist changes and have difficulty with life transitions. Fear of change is pervasive and can render successful people powerless and powerful people helpless. It is sad but too often true that everyone wants a better life, but no one wants to change.

What is it that leads people to fear and resist that which is new? It begins very early in life as evidenced by a brief exchange I had with my seven-year-old son the other day. We were sitting out on our back patio and I was looking over a flyer from the town recreation department. I started reading aloud to him about a summer camp program, describing the exciting adventures and activities he might enjoy.

"I'm not going!" he firmly asserted.

"Why not?" I asked.

"I don't like it!"

There you have it. I don't know what it is, I have never done it, seen it nor even discussed it in any great detail, but I assure you, I don't like it! How many of us fall victim to this unconscious, yet powerful force in our mind that says, "If it's new and unknown, I don't like it"?

The phrase "fear of change" is actually somewhat of a misnomer for it is actually anxiety that we feel when we think about pending changes. Anxiety and fear are often lumped together but are truly two different emotions.

Fear is what you feel when you are being chased through the woods by a big, hairy grizzly bear. Your heart races, your adrenalin pumps through your body, and your senses are elevated. You are on alert and ready to act. *Anxiety* on the other hand is like a hyperactive watchdog. It never comes to rest, is always on alert and a bit too jumpy. It reacts to anything that goes bump in the night, or day, or any other time for that matter. Anxiety never lets you rest. It fills your mind with pending doom. It is the all-pervasive "what if's" that never end. It is truly anxiety – facing the great unknown – that leads to avoiding change.

General anxiety about change consists of a conglomerate of other anxieties that we have come to call fears such as:

> Fear of failure or conversely fear of success
> Fear of what others will think of me
> Fear of choosing something that is unpleasant
> Fear of upsetting others
> Fear of loss
> Fear of discomfort or that the new endeavor will be too hard
> Fear of the unknown

Another manifestation of the anxiety involved with life transitions is self-doubt. When faced with new and uncertain territory, we can be riddled with worries about our skills, competence and capacities. Thoughts like, "What if I'm not good (smart, skilled, experienced) enough" can often race through one's mind and literally render you powerless over taking planned, thoughtful, prudent action.

5. Change as Vulnerability

Perhaps one of the most challenging aspects of adapting to change is the degree of vulnerability that it creates. It is common to feel a loss of control when life is changing, particularly when a change has been sudden and unplanned. But even with planned change, there is a sense of vulnerability with the newness and the unknown. We live under the illusion that we are in control of our lives. I say "illusion" because we are constantly at the whims of life and change, but we largely live as if all of our plans will work out, our goals will succeed, our cars won't break down, our basements won't flood and our children won't go through the terrible twos or teens. Of course, we live as though we are in control – to live any other way would leave us feeling constantly frightened, anxious and even immobilized. The children's movie "Finding Nemo" is a wonderfully sweet depiction of the fears we all could face, and the degree to which we could be held captive by those fears if we allowed ourselves to delve into the stark reality that scores of really bad things happen to really good people every day. We can't function with all of these grim possibilities, so we move along believing that our lives are going to work out just fine.

The vulnerability I am talking about is when something happens that leaves us feeling exposed, when we need something from someone else or when we are not able to independently care for ourselves. Children and the elderly are vulnerable due to their ongoing need for care and assistance. We are vulnerable when our feelings get hurt; when we have tried something new and watch our efforts fail. We are vulnerable when we are lost – either literally or figuratively. Vulnerability makes you want to run and hide, to curl into a self-protective cocoon and not let others in.

We too often relate to vulnerability as weakness, thus our tendency to fear change – for fear that the change will leave us vulnerable, lost, uncertain, exposed and therefore weak.

Dr. Brené Brown, a research professor at the University of Houston Graduate School of Social Work, gave a wonderful lecture on the concept of vulnerability based on her own social science research and found that vulnerability in fact leads to tremendous personal and relational strength. She talked about people who demonstrate vulnerability as the willingness and ability "to say 'I love you' first, the willingness to do something where there are no guarantees, the willingness to breathe through waiting for the doctor to call after your mammogram. They're willing to invest in a relationship that may or may not work out."[4]

Change that involves loss often leaves us feeling vulnerable. We no longer have what was lost to hold onto and give us a sense of grounding in the world. Change that involves new goals or direction in life leaves us feeling vulnerable because we are "sticking our neck out," trying something new and heaven forbid we should change our mind, or worse yet – fail! When we consider taking on a new goal or direction, all too often our ego minds kick in with a round of disparaging rants, "What will they think of me? Why was I so stupid? What was I thinking?" And on and on our mind goes, tormenting us with all manner of unpleasant thought and emotion. This inner torment is the vulnerability we often face when we embark on a path of change.

To combat our ongoing sense of vulnerability, recent social and neuroscience research points to the fact that many people experience "optimism bias" which means that one believes that they are less at risk of experiencing a negative event compared to others. We think things will be better in the future than in the past, and in general we tend to anticipate that things will turn out better than they do. Optimism bias is one of our best defenses against the vulnerability we feel in the face of life's inevitable changes.
Thinking "it will all be ok" or in fact, even better than it is now (whatever the "it" may be at the moment) helps us face the

---

4. (http://www.ted.com/talks/brene_brown_on_vulnerability.html)

uncertainty of change with a sense of hope and power.

A study done by the Mayo clinic in Minnesota studied the levels of optimism versus pessimism in 839 people over a 30-year span. The study found that those who scored higher on the optimism scale actually lived longer! The study showed that every 10-point increase in pessimism correlated with a 19% increase in death rate.

Optimism bias helps us to be resilient in the face of challenge, tragedy and trauma. It helps us feel hopeful, and hope gives rise to possibility. Look at the tragic happenings that occurred in New Orleans in August of 2005 when Hurricane Katrina and the subsequent floods devastated an entire city, or the 2010 earthquake that decimated Haiti leaving hundreds of thousands of people homeless, without food, water and medical care.

In both of these natural disasters, there were numerous reports of people's spirits rising to the call and asserting that they would rebuild, come back stronger and overcome the tragedy. Whether or not this is actually the case is less important than the hope and strength that is drawn from a sense of optimism in the face of tragedy and radical life change.

Optimism bias can be seen both as a defense against the powerlessness and vulnerability of change or also as a belief system. I, for one, have been accused more than once of being more optimistic than realistic and I would say my life is better for it. I don't want to settle for what is merely reasonable or realistic in life. I want to believe in miracles and look for them. I want to see the partly cloudy day as mostly sunny. It's a big world out there, with lots of change that comes our way and I want to take it all on as if every turn that comes my way is certainly a blessing – sometimes bright and shining as the day, sometimes in disguise – but a blessing just the same.

Summary:

With all of this difficulty with change, why would any of us venture out beyond our familiar and comfortable life to the great unknown? Despite the anxiety with things that are new, fear of things that are unknown and vulnerability with feeling exposed, we still engage with life in a sense of curiosity, exploration and adventure. We desire to master our own destiny and to give rise to new possibilities. We long to explore, to connect, to contribute. We are relational beings who grow and transform as we allow ourselves the gift of awareness and change. Thus, we face our fears and grow beyond what once had stopped us. That is a very good thing, because it leads us ever into the fullness of life, embracing the promise of change.

Chapter Four: The Promise of Change

I would be remiss if I wrote this whole book on change and only addressed the difficult aspects. I have devoted my entire career to understanding human potential, growth and change. It is something I am passionate about mastering and helping others do the same. I strongly believe that with awareness and commitment, we can train ourselves to master life's challenges and opportunities. Dealing with life change represents both challenge and opportunity.

Every year I teach a six-month personal growth coaching program called *Life Design*. The intention of the course is to deeply examine the way you live your life and evaluate the way you are living relative to your core values and dreams, and then begin redesigning your life to begin matching up to the image in your mind's eye for how you truly want your life to be. In other words, it is an intensive on creating life change.

The people who take this course are from all walks of life. I have had ministers, physicians, software engineers, teachers, veterinarians, social workers and business owners in the course. The course is not designed for a particular field or set of beliefs. It is designed for people who are interested in getting more out of life, and giving more to life. I often say that it is for success-oriented people who are up to something.

In the course people examine the difference between living life by default, which is when you are living primarily in response to what comes your way, versus living life by design, which is when you intentionally seek to create and manifest the results and outcomes – in other words, the *changes*, that you want to bring forth in your life.

In the process of this course I have seen people get married, get divorced, buy new homes and sell old ones, purchase retirement property and downsize to own a lot less of everything. Some people have started businesses while others sold or ended them. Houses, offices, attics and closets get cleaned out. One participant literally removed over a ton of paper from his home office! Enormous changes get generated in the process of the program – all in keeping with the course intention of living life by design rather than by default.

Think about it for a moment. If you were truly to begin designing your life the way you wanted it to be, what would you do? What would it look like? How would your relationships be impacted? What about your career? Most people don't take on such an arduous task because they simply don't know where to begin. They lack the support, the blueprint or perhaps the courage to take apart their life and reconstruct one that is a better fit and feel. That is the magic of the program – it provides all of that for those who are willing to stand up and say that they are ready to live their life with intention, clarity, and courage; to being living life by design.

Having designed and instructed this program for as long as I have, as well as being a coach and therapist for so long, I have seen first-hand both the challenge and the promise of change. I have seen lives truly transformed. This is the possibility and the promise of change.

One of the participants told me upon registering for the course that she had wanted to take it for the past three of four years, but she was too afraid to do so. She said that she knew that taking this course would ensure that she would make the changes in her life that she had wanted to make for a long time, but was simply too afraid to begin. Once in the structure of the program, however, she befriended change and took on the things she had been avoiding for far too long. She recognized the important truth that external change that is not grounded in inner wisdom, vision and purpose will not lead to a greater life. Anyone can create change – the question remains as to whether you are going to create change that is inspired by something deeper within you, with awareness and clarity of purpose or merely create chaos to avoid a current unpleasant reality.

There is a phrase that is used among therapists that describes some people's tendency to move to a new location, or change jobs when they are feeling some type of inner angst in life. The phrase is "the geographical cure." It is used by those who seek some relief of inner discomfort by changing external circumstances. Of course, what eventually shows up again, after the newness and uncertainty of the external change has died down, is the same inner angst or discomfort that prompted the move in the first place. This sort of "change-for-change-sake" decision making leads to a life of turmoil and chaos rather than a life of thoughtful, planned, inner-guided living.

Intentional change or living life by design is a powerful and fulfilling way to move through life. It creates an inner reservoir of strength, confidence, clarity and internal power that is second to none and can be developed and strengthened by recognizing the promise of mastering change.

A. Mastering Change Provides Greater Opportunities to Grow

This whole notion of personal growth has been on the brunt end of too much bad Saturday night comedy and mindless sitcoms. The depth and importance of personal growth work has lost any sense of sacredness or honor, which is unfortunate since the most powerful opportunity we have in life is to grow. By personal growth, I mean to develop broader perceptions, to expand your knowledge, to experience a greater tolerance for things different from you and what you are accustomed to, to be aware of your beliefs, values, biases and fears so that you may make better choices. Personal growth allows you to develop the capacity to reflect on your own perceptions and see where they may be limiting you.

The path of personal growth is one that takes your swimming pool and turns it into an ocean. The more you are able to develop your change tolerance, the more you can face life and stay strong, centered and ready to embrace your experience. You can look at different aspects of life and call it good rather than shrink away from it out of fear. The more you increase your tolerance for change, the more of life you can embrace, experience, contribute and know.

Those who are highly change averse may be limited by difficulty embracing that which is new and unfamiliar. This is not necessarily bad, it is merely limiting. I define *personal freedom* as having the most choices and options available to you with regard to what is important to you. Not just choice for choice sake (that can be overwhelming!), but choice about what really matters. Choice in how you live, what people you engage with, what difference you make in the world, what you do for fun and leisure, and what you are willing to try. The greater the choices you are able to consider, the greater freedom you have.

As a therapist when I work with people who are experiencing anxiety regarding change, I encourage them to simply get the information needed to at least consider the change – such as go to the gym and get a tour, call the admissions office and see what the requirements are, or complete the résumé to prepare for the next step of the job search. Making small, incremental changes can be a way to ease into next steps and greater options, and therefore greater freedom. The more you can adapt to change, the more you can grow.

B. Mastering Change Aids Your Resiliency

Resiliency is a sense of inner strength and the feeling that you can get through anything. Mastering change and increasing your change tolerance aids to your resiliency by knowing that you have the resources needed to face and embrace change. You know that you can adapt, get support, and establish new paradigms, perspectives and ways of doing things in life and therefore you are less apt to live in a self-protected cocoon, hoping that the winds of change do not come your way.

I remember going through a really bad break up back in my twenty's. It was one of those break-ups that no one saw coming. I thought we were doing great. We were planning on moving in together and really settling into a lovely lifestyle after a wonderful five years together. Then the dreaded "I'm not in love with you any longer" came my way. Oh how I hate that phrase. To this day, I cringe when I hear friends who are on the receiving end of that chilling sentence. The break-up was sudden and oh-so-final. I was devastated.

Realizing that it would take me awhile to get through this unexpected loss, I was very gentle with myself in those first few days and weeks. I took almost a full week off from work and wandered aimlessly through shopping malls and sat in a daze in movie theatres or sporting arenas. I spent time with close friends who seemed to never tire of my tears. I went on a spontaneous weekend get-away to Paris. I really let myself grieve and adapt to this huge, unplanned life change.

After the dust settled, and I began to create my "new normal" I was left with a solid knowing that if I could get through that experience, I could get through anything. It became my measure of comparison when other painful unplanned changes came my way. I developed a new sense of identity that said, "If I can get through that with my sense of self intact, I can get through anything." And indeed, I most certainly have. As the saying goes, "That which doesn't kill you will make you stronger!" This is true of learning to adapt to life change as well.

C. Mastering Change Provides the Opportunity for a Better Life

Having the ability to plan, execute and tolerate life change opens doors to explore creating a better life than the one you currently have. Even when the life you currently have is good, even great, you can always seek to expand your current experience.

One of my Life Design students, Donna, had a lovely life; married with two adorable children, working full time in a high-level management job, financially comfortable and from an outside view, Donna looked like she "had it all." But on the inside, she was suffering and unfulfilled. She loved her children and spouse, but felt burdened by the constant demands of working full time and caring for the family and home. During the course of Life Design, she realized that she had been avoiding big areas of her life due to her fear of change. Despite the fact that she was a former skilled and successful athlete, she had gained 30 pounds since becoming a parent, her house was in constant disarray and she was spending almost no quality time with her children and spouse. She realized that if she was going to create a life by design, rather than continuing in her survival mode, she needed to make some drastic changes. She saw that her job was the biggest drain on her time and that she really did not feel any sense of connection to the work or fulfillment from what she was doing. She had long wanted to be a counselor or coach, but felt afraid to make such a drastic change. Over the course of the next year, she approached her husband about her feelings and they created a plan where Donna would cut back to part time at her work, get a coaching certification and then within a year, she would leave her job completely. She was totally energized with her new passion for coaching. Because Donna felt supported and energized by her new decisions, she also formed a workout group with some friends and started doing in-home exercise classes with a video program. She was leading the group, so this inspired her even further to begin eating better, and she soon began dropping the weight she had gained.

Donna recognized that once she decided to step into her fears of upsetting the family life, leaving her job, and starting a new venture, she was actually much happier and fulfilled. Her kids were thrilled with the changes, because while it meant they did not have the same level of financial comfort, they had a mom who was excited and enthused about her life. It all began with Donna's decision to begin mastering change and put the change process to work for the better.

D. Mastering Change Allows You to do More Good

My mom is not someone who I would say is a master of change. She is similar to my Uncle Mike – having lived in the same zip code almost her entire life, working at the same types of jobs, spending time with the same friends forever. She's a lovely woman – she's the first one at the door with a casserole when there's been a death in someone's family; she drives 95 year-old Millie to her doctor's appointments and to get her hair done; she cleans the church and visits the sick in the hospital as part of the church outreach ministry. You could easily say that my mom does a lot of good in the world at the level at which she is comfortable creating life change (which in her case means keeping things desperately the same). Just think about what she might have done is she ever mastered creating intentional change! That is not to diminish her contributions to her community in one bit. But it's a big world out there, and there is such tremendous need. One of the reasons I am passionate about helping people master and create intentional life change is that for those who have the capacity and inclination to give and contribute in life should do so to the highest and best of their abilities. The more we grow in our capacity to create change, the more good we all can do. As Mother Teresa of Calcutta is quoted, "We cannot all do great things, but we can do small things with great love."

A dear friend of mine was so compelled by wanting to do more for the world that she learned how to navigate a sea of change, take on tremendous personal growth and was able to create a tremendous legacy of good. Shipley Allinson was running her own macrobiotic restaurant and raising two children when she felt called to do more and bring her spiritual awareness to others. She started a small study group in her home, studying the practical spiritual principles of the Unity church. She later went on to gain her ministerial degree and founded a Unity church, Unity on the River, in Amesbury, Massachusetts. Over the past 15 years she has provided the leadership and vision to grow the church to be a vibrant beacon of light for people seeking spiritual fulfillment. While this story is inspiring and compelling, it becomes more so with the added fact that Shipley is a raging introvert who was terrified of public speaking. She began doing her weekly talks by using 3 by 5 cards, and basically reading her notes. Today she is one of the most dynamic and talented ministers I have ever heard, leading congregations of 200 or more every Sunday with inspiring, engaging and deeply moving spiritual messages.

The more we are willing to take on and master change, the more we can have a positive impact and serve the greater good in the world.

E. Mastering Change Makes You Happier

The ability to adapt to change, roll with what life brings us and take risks makes our lives so much richer and expansive. I am expressing a value in this statement – my value that "it's a big world out there" and we are here to enjoy it. Part of enjoying life means that you are able to pursue what is meaningful and important to you. I teach a holistically oriented productivity course in which I define productivity as making clear, consistent progress toward that which is important to you. I believe that it is in being productive and actively engaged in life that we experience our greatest joy. In fact, there are all kinds of studies that show that when people no longer have anything to take care of, be engaged in or find meaning in, their rates of mortality skyrocket. Give an elderly person in a nursing home a plant to tend to and they live longer. We are born to be active and engaged. Life is active, and in fact, always changing. So the more we master the change process, the more fully and deeply we can express ourselves and pursue what matters.

Pursuing what matters to you will, on some level, involve setting goals. Whether your goals are formally thought out, written down, with a step-by-step plan or merely provide you with a sense of direction and meaning, having goals is a big part of our overall happiness and psychic wellbeing. Conventional wisdom might lead you to believe that it is the achievement of a goal that leads to greater happiness and satisfaction, but current social science research is pointing to something quite different. Research has found that it is the process of striving toward a goal, rather than attaining the goal, that leads to sustained happiness.[5]

I found this to be quite counter-intuitive at first, until I mapped this research onto my own experience. I reflected on times that I had achieved some major accomplishment – such as the completion of

---

5. Tal Ben-Shahar, Ph.D., *Happier: Learn the Secrets to Daily Joy and Lasting Fulfillment,* 2007).

graduate school or establishing a new service program within an organization, purchasing my home – the actual accomplishment of these goals was often met with a temporary raise in satisfaction, but soon there was a tremendous let down and a feeling of "now what?" I believe we are wired for growth and development and then when we stop growing, pursuing, achieving things – even the most mundane of accomplishments – then we start to die.

People wanting to take on the pursuit of goals as part of mastering change should be aware that it is the pursuit of intrinsically meaningful goals that involve personal growth, connection and contribution rather than externally motivated goals such as the pursuit of wealth, power and fame that lead to greater happiness and fulfillment. I have had many coaching clients who said they wanted to hire me to double their sales or to reach financial independence. When leading them on an inquiry regarding the origin of such a goal, what they were each seeking was some sense of greater ease, freedom of time and ability to contribute to others. This can be accomplished with our without financial freedom. Focusing on the external goal would not lead to fulfillment. Far too often when one doubles their income, they unconsciously double their expenditures as well – leading to a vicious cycle of striving without ever achieving what was sought, because what was sought was an internal condition, not an external circumstance.

Summary:

We have covered the exciting promise of change. The possibilities above are available when we train ourselves to master the life change process. I say "train ourselves" because adapting to and initiating life change is a skill that can be learned. That means there are specific actions that when consistently employed, will increase your skill and capacity to roll with life's turns. In the next chapter (for those of you who haven't already jumped ahead!), we will go into the skills and practices that create a mastery in dealing with life change.

Chapter Five: What To Do About Change

Part 1

I am writing this chapter sitting on the deck at my great aunt's cottage that I mentioned in the introduction. While I have owned it for the past four years, somehow I still refer to this little cottage as being my great aunt's. I know I own it now. I live here 3 months out of the year and have done little things to make it my own. Nevertheless, the sense of it belonging to a time, place and person from a time before I was born grounds me in a comforting and familiar way.

I have made some big decisions in my life that have allowed me to maintain a sense of familiarity in my world and some that have had just the opposite effect. That really is the crux of life, isn't it? We spend our days and our years bouncing back and forth between the familiar and the unknown, or between what French sociologist Emile Durkheim referred to as between the sacred and the profane. The sacred being that quality of life that has "otherworldliness" to it, an ethereal, larger-than-life quality, while the profane is the ordinary, everydayness of life that we all encounter. Thus is our charge as human beings, living our lives in a mystical dance between the sacred and the profane.

It is in mastering life change, or better yet, our response to the inevitable, sometimes hospitable, sometimes unthinkable changes that gives us a sense of personal power, confidence and ability to dwell more deeply in the sacred rather than the profane.

In this chapter, I want to look at two different ways we have to deal with this little problem of "what to do about change." The first of these relates to the best ways to respond when change comes our way. There are certain ways that you can strengthen your navigation skills so that you meet the winds of change with greater strength, clarity and direction.

The next section will address what to do about change that you want to initiate in our life, but have been unsuccessful in creating. What is it that makes creating sustained change so difficult? From losing weight, to starting a new exercise program and eating more healthy or starting a new business – we often seem like we are a prisoner to our old habits and ways of being. This section will provide some understanding and strategies for what to do to create long-lasting, meaningful change.

I will present to you ten keys to mastering change, which will enhance your ability to master life since life is all about growth and change. As you go through this chapter, be sure that you call to mind the changes that you are facing or those that have troubled you in the past, so that you make the material real and vital to your personal experience. No short primer on change will set you up for a lifetime of total ease. Life doesn't work that way. It is rich, complex and challenging and certainly not in our total control. But the more we learn about how to roll with the vicissitudes of life, the more we will emerge strong and confident that we can take whatever life sends our way, and know that we will not only survive, but thrive. We can come to realize that our lives are not merely about what we accomplish and acquire, but what we contributed along the way, about how we felt through the process and the way we impacted others. There is no laboratory that can adequately teach such hard-won lessons. Your life consciously lived and intentionally designed, is your laboratory.

A. Change as the Uninvited Guest

In some ways writing about how to manage change that comes to us uninvited is really just silly. I mean, life is always changing. When I started this book, my son was a six-year-old first grader and now he's a seven-year-old second grader (a fact that he is quick to announce these days!). I was living in Lexington, Massachusetts and now I am living in Morristown, NY (my hometown and where Aunt Kitty's cottage – I mean MY cottage resides). I was looking forward to speaking at a national convention in Detroit, which is now just a pleasant memory. When I began this book, my friend Mary's dad was healthy and going to work every day, now he is resting at home with Stage IV cancer and likely is enjoying his last summer with his family and friends. Change is a given. Yet we get our shirts tied up in a knot about this thing called change all the time. Sometimes change happens rapidly and leaves our head spinning, sometimes life lulls us into the comfortable notion that things may always stay the same. But we know better. The tides of change will come our way and the best we can do is prepare ourselves for the inevitable, wonderful, frightful, delicious, unnerving sea of change.

Preparing for the unknown is somewhat of an oxymoron, I know. But when learning to do anything well, you have to learn a skill set or behavior and then practice it. You want to create a level of knowing deep within that you can reliably replicate that skill or behavior, regardless of circumstances. As a younger athlete who played college basketball, I shot free throws with 89 percent accuracy. I did not randomly develop that skill. I stood at the free throw line shooting hundreds of free throws, running sprints, and then shooting more. I would visualize each element of my shot, from the dribble of the ball, to the bending of the knees to the flick of my wrist and then the "swoosh" of the net as the ball breezed through. My friend and racquetball coach, Fran Davis, was once the top female player in the world. She would stay on the court hitting literally thousands of shots down the line, cross-court and to the ceiling, meticulously keeping her statistics on placing the ball exactly where she wanted it to go. In order to master anything, you must be willing to put in the work that excellence demands.

Do you know that the rate of airplane accidents due to human error had been consistent for somewhere around 40 years, despite increased training, greater time off, longer rest periods and any other human intervention that the aviation industry could conjure up? Then suddenly in 1990 a drastic improvement occurred. Why? Flight simulators were invented. That's right, flight simulators. After 1990 pilots had the opportunity to learn new skills by practicing the concepts in real-time simulation, not just learning them with paper and ink. Revolutionary!

The same is true for mastering change – the more you can take the concept and turn it into an experience – simulated or otherwise - the more you will master the skill of adapting to change. By *mastering change*, I mean facing what comes your way with a sense of equanimity, purpose, poise and grace, to end up stronger and better for having gone through the change rather than being left angry, weakened and devastated. Some people are naturally more resilient, and some have to work at it. For those of us who need to work at it (and I include myself firmly in that category!), knowing what to do, what to work on, what skills to develop is a tremendous asset in mastering change.

B. They Called Her *Grace*

Grace Nichols Woodside was my paternal grandmother. A warm woman, slight in stature but strong in spirit. She was and will always be my greatest role model for dealing with change as an uninvited guest with grace and poise. There are times when change brings unthinkable and tragic circumstances our way, and yet it is always up to us how we respond to these harsh realities.

In 1965, Grace experienced the unthinkable – circumstances that would have taken many down. In May of that year, Grace's eldest son, Jack - my father and namesake – was killed in a car crash. Married with three young children, he was taken in an instant. The town was shaken and Grace was distraught as any mother would be. In an almost unimaginable turn, six months later, Grace's youngest son, Harry Alfred was also killed in a car crash. Harry was a young, vibrant, handsome and athletic young man with a beautiful fiancée and bright future ahead of him. The community showered their sympathy and support upon my mother for the loss of her husband and my grandmother who had lost two of her three sons. People were shocked to see such tragedy befall one woman in such a short period of time. But Grace carried on – channeling her grief into her love of her three grandchildren (and for this I remain eternally grateful). And yet tragedy stopped at her door yet again. Nine months after burying her two sons, Grace's husband, too, was killed in an automobile accident. In nine months' time, Grace lost her husband and two sons tragically and unexpectedly.

Nine years passed and Grace found her way through her grief by caring for her grandchildren, working at the local school as the librarian, and helping out at her church and running the annual Cancer Society and Easter Seals fund drives. She was a strong woman with a loving heart filled with grace. After 9 years of being widowed, her college roommate, Janet, fell ill with cancer and as it became clear that she was going to make her transition, she began to tell her husband, Harold, "I want you to go find Grace Woodside. She is a lovely woman and she is lonely. You will need a good woman and she doesn't deserve such loneliness. She has had such loss in her life. I don't want you to be alone and you two will be good for one another. Go find Grace when I am gone."

Janet passed away and Harold waited a few months of mourning before he made the call. But soon enough, he and my grandmother were the most precious couple, going everywhere together, doing projects, taking small trips here and there. In very short order, Harold proposed and my grandmother remarried. It was a sweet ceremony held in Grandma's living room with just the family attending. Harold was a wonderful addition to our family. He adored my grandmother and they were wonderful companions.

I hesitate to even begin this next paragraph – partly because it is so painful to recall, partly because I disdain showering this grief on you, and partly because I think you wouldn't believe such tragedy could befall one person – but within a year of their marriage tragedy struck again. While Harold's son, Bob, was visiting over Labor Day weekend, he and his wife joined Grace's remaining son, my Uncle Tom and his wife, to go out for the evening. On their way home, yet another car accident occurred and Harold's son, Bob, who was married with two young children, was killed.

There are so many ways one could respond to such tragedy, such unanticipated and unimaginable life change. It was my grandmother's response to these life tragedies that left their mark me and on so many others for years to come. At her funeral and wake over twenty years later, the room where Grandma laid was packed. People whom I had not seen in over two decades came to pay their respects. Over and over again, what I heard was, "She was such a remarkable woman," "She went through so much tragedy but yet always had something to give others," "Her pies were the best and she always seemed to have fresh cookies in the jar. We would go for a walk in the evening hoping Grace would be out on the porch because we knew she would invite us up for a piece of pie or some dessert." Loving, giving, gracious – those are words that described Grace's character and way of being. They transcended her life of unthinkable tragedy and became her legacy.

Having Grandma Grace's presence and love as part of my life was perhaps the most powerful influence in developing my sense of resilience and belief that while we cannot control everything that happens to us, we can – with faith and a little grace – determine how we respond to the things that life brings our way. I have spent most of my life helping people adapt to change – either that which was uninvited or that which people wanted to initiate. Here are the ten elements that I have found to be instrumental in mastering life change when change is the uninvited guest.

C. Ten Elements for Mastering Change

1. Practice acceptance. Millions of people in the recovery movement have been comforted and found strength in a simple truism known as "The Serenity Prayer." The simplicity, ease and wisdom of this immortal prayer helped countless souls find peace and acceptance amid the difficulty and strife of recovery from addiction. The prayer is this:

> *"God grant me the serenity to accept the things I cannot change,*
> *the courage to change the things I can,*
> *and the wisdom to know the difference."*

It is true that while we can influence a great deal about what happens in our lives through our actions, work ethic, beliefs, personal growth and relationships that we cultivate, we cannot control every occurrence or event in our lives. People like my grandmother are testaments to that truth, as are people like Gabrielle Giffords who was shot in the head during a rogue assassination attempt in Arizona in 2011, or Christopher Reeve who after a career as a Super Hero, became quadriplegic after a horseback riding accident. Unexpected change happens. Tragedy strikes. Everyone I can think of has been faced with some form of adversity. It is simply a part of life and the more you are able and willing to surrender yourself to that fact, the easier it will be for you to give yourself over to the wisdom of this simple prayer.
There is an odd comfort in the unity we feel with others who know our pain, who have faced our suffering. The truth is, all who live also suffer. It is part of the human experience and the more we embrace that fact, the greater comfort we can feel amid our difficulties.

What is happening in your life today that bringing acceptance would soften? What old wounds are you carrying that if you brought acceptance to the memory of this experience, some of your wounding may heal? I was having lunch with a friend last week who was still angry about her son having failed first grade – and her son is now a senior in high school! That is a long time to carry anger or a grudge when the simple act of acceptance would bring such greater ease and grace, not to mention peace of mind.

2. Be gentle with yourself. Recognize that change is hard, especially those changes that we do not invite or initiate into our lives. Change can leave you feeling anxious, vulnerable, uncertain and with a loss of confidence to face your life. Such difficult times call for compassion. *Self-compassion* is a highly underrated personal skill and trait. We are a very driven culture and one that values being able to "tough it out" and "go it alone." This is so totally contrary to human nature. We all want to help others and often are able to show compassion for those who are suffering adversity. So why do we not bring this compassion home to our own heart and soul?

My client, Leslie, a mid-50's single mother who, in the span of a few short months became her mother's caretaker as she recovered from cancer, and her adolescent son had a psychotic episode (a serious mental health condition). She was overwhelmed with her responsibilities, learning how to navigate both the health care system to advocate for her mother, and the juvenile mental health system to get help for her son. She was taking so much time off work that eventually it was necessary for her to leave her well-paying corporate job in the middle of the worst recession in our generation. Leslie hired me as her coach about a year after these two life-changing events occurred when she wanted to begin looking for a job. She was having trouble motivating herself, felt overwhelmed, lacked confidence and clarity about her direction. She felt like she had let her children down during her years of working in the corporate sector and being a single mother. Her inner dialogue was incredibly harsh and she was placing enormous pressure on herself to "hurry up and find a job." While it was my commitment as her coach to help her accomplish her stated goal, it was also my commitment that she do so with a sense of wellbeing and balance. So my first charge to her was this simple treaty, "Be gentle with yourself." Leslie was astonished at this notion. She had been pushing herself so hard, scheduling every minute meeting with either health care practitioners or various mental health providers, looking online for jobs, going to networking events, caring for her house and other child that she had not taken a moment to think about *her* needs in this process. I had her begin thinking about how she wanted this next phase of her life to be, taking some time every day to do something fun and relaxing, and starting to get better sleep. I encouraged her to use this simple phrase, "Be gentle with yourself" throughout the day to remind herself that she did not have to push so hard. She started seeing a therapist to offer more emotional support for her anxiety and finally began to recognize the emotional, financial and psychological toll these unexpected changes had brought into her life. She cried, got mad, and allowed herself to grieve. It was a necessary first step that allowed her to move forward with her job search with a clear sense of what she wanted and a belief that she could actually have it. She knew that she no longer wanted to be in a high-pressured, demanding corporate environment, nor did she want to engage in a long commute into the city for her job. As she honed in on her desires, she was bolstered in her enthusiasm to create a more balanced life. She had to endure the anxiety of saying "no" to those jobs that did not meet her definition of being gentle with herself. It took several months for Leslie to land the job she wanted, but once she did, she was elated to see that with a commitment to her wellbeing and clarity about what she wanted to create, she really could impact the direction her life would take – one where she was both earning a satisfying income, doing work she enjoyed and being able to respond to the needs of her mother and son.

In what areas of your life do you need to be gentle with yourself? Where are you pushing yourself too hard and not honoring a sane pace and harmonious rhythm? Take a moment now to imagine what it would look like to begin being more gentle with yourself. Would you go to bed earlier? Sleep in a bit later? Would you leave your desk at lunch to take a much-needed stretch and walk? Would you start seeing a counselor or hire a coach? What can you do today that is being gentle with yourself?

Feel free to use the punch list in Appendix A as a simple reminder of the ways you can practice this important element.

3. Identify your values. Leslie's story highlights another important component regarding mastering unexpected change. Knowing what you value, what you care about, what lights you up and what you want in your life is essential when you are facing life's unexpected turns. Identifying one's core values is a fundamental process in my Life Design course. Identifying your core values must occur if you are to being intentionally crafting your life in line with what really matters to you, in alignment with what you love and are here to accomplish and fulfill.

While identifying your values may seem like a simple process, many people become very perplexed at honing in on the five or six core elements of their life. In my courses I offer simple inventories to guide your discernment of what is most important to you. This awareness fuels the flame of creativity and personal power. Below are two exercises to help you clarify and identify your core values.

In order to align your behaviors, decisions and actions with what is most important to you, you need to determine and articulate your fundamental values. Your values are the qualities and characteristics that you want to define your life. This exercise is designed to help you do so. Answer the questions below to begin discerning your core values:

a. Identify five people who you admire, either living or dead, whom you know or have never met.

b. List one or more qualities and characteristics you most admire for each person.

c. List five qualities or characteristics you most appreciate about yourself.

d. List three to five topics you get very passionate when I talk or think about when you think or talk about that topic.

e. Look at the lists above, and notice areas of repetition. What things do you admire in yourself AND in others? What things that you care about in yourself and others are also a part of what you are passionate about? Is there overlap? Use this as a guide to determining what you truly value. The qualities and characteristics you value in others are often what you want to express. Based on this exploration, discern and write your five top values here.

For some, a more linear, left-brain approach to inner work is more useful. So to help further discern the unique, personal values with which you want to align your energy and resources, select five values below to be identified as your core values. You may want to begin by choosing 10 or more and then from that smaller list, choose your top five. Remember, these are all good things, so it's not that you don't want "knowledge" or "loyalty" in your life. The question is what do you want to be the core or defining element of your life? What do you want to declare as the fundamental guiding principles in your life and what characteristics do you want to be a part of your personal legacy?

Values

☐ Achievement/Accomplishment	☐ Knowledge
☐ Adventure	☐ Leadership
☐ Alignment/Living your values	☐ Loving kindness
☐ Art	☐ Loyalty
☐ Authenticity	☐ Mindful living
☐ Autonomy	☐ Nurturing
☐ Beauty and aesthetics	☐ Order/Organization
☐ Belonging/Community	☐ Peace and tranquility
☐ Collaboration	☐ Planning
☐ Contribution/Service	☐ Playfulness
☐ Commitment	☐ Prayer
☐ Communication skills	☐ Personal power
☐ Earning power (Financial)	☐ Recognition
☐ Empowerment	☐ Results
☐ Enjoyment/Fun	☐ Risk taking
☐ Entertainment (TV, theatre, etc.)	☐ Romance/Intimacy
☐ Environmental sustainability	☐ Science/Exploration
☐ Excellence/Mastery	☐ Security
☐ Family	☐ Self-expression
☐ Financial freedom	☐ Service to others
☐ Faith	☐ Solitude
☐ Freedom	☐ Success
☐ Generosity	☐ Spiritual growth
☐ Gratitude	☐ Spontaneity
☐ Growth and learning	☐ Tradition
☐ Health, wellness, fitness	☐ Transcendence
☐ Honesty	☐ Vitality/Zeal
☐ Humor	☐ Wealth
☐ Integrity/Being your word	☐ Wonder
☐ Justice	☐ Other:

Write those FIVE VALUES here:

1. _____

2. _____

3. _____

4. _____

5. _____

Values Clarification Completion

Compare the two lists from the two previous exercises here:

What do you see? What similarities are expressed or what themes emerged?

From the two lists above, choose five of these items and establish these as your core values!

MY FIVE CORE VALUES ARE:

1. _____

2. _____

3. _____

4. _____

5. _____

4. Have faith in yourself. Allow the knowledge that you have survived previous life changes bolster you against the current winds of change. Wherever you are in your life, you have indeed handled life's twists and turns up to this point. Let the failures you have endured teach you about yourself. The knowledge that you have emerged stronger and wiser from your setbacks can create an inner reservoir of confidence and certainty that you can handle whatever life throws at you. You are not a novice at this. You have some traction. Believing in yourself, in your resiliency and in your ability to get through things is a tremendous asset in facing change.

5. Have faith in something larger than yourself. There is such tremendous wisdom in the recovery program called "The 12-Steps." I'm sure you have heard of these programs, participated in them or know someone who has. The most popular and well known is Alcoholics Anonymous or AA, but there are recovery programs for every possible addiction from gambling to sex and love to under earning and over eating. Perhaps the most elemental component to this recovery model is for each person to identity a belief in something greater than himself or herself – what they call in the program your "higher power." Bob, a therapy client who was early in recovery, said that one of the "old timer" AA members, a man with a long history of sobriety and a lot of experience in the program told Bob, "I don't care what your higher power is. It can be that old maple tree out there, it can be the mountain you climbed last weekend or it can be the doorknob you used to come into this room. I don't care what you choose to believe in, but you have got to believe in something greater than yourself."

Science has proven the primordial wisdom that Bill Wilson, the founder of AA, established back in 1935. In their book, "How God Changes Your Brain," neuroscientists Andrew Newberg and Mark Robert Waldman indicate that faith in something greater than you is the best way to have a healthy brain, to feel better, be happier and to roll with the winds of change. Newberg says, "To me, it doesn't matter if God is an illusion or fact, because even as a metaphor, God represents all we are capable of becoming, an ideal that offers hope to millions of people…Faith in an optimistic future may be a placebo, but it's important to remember that placebos can cure, on average, 20 percent of most medical and emotional diseases." Faith or belief in something larger than you can be tremendously soothing in times of loss, change and transition. When I was young, the thought of faith meant very little to me. I was raised in a Catholic home and faith was something that was a part of our family culture much the way sports and certain family recipes were imbued in our family. Faith in my early years was not necessarily personal, intimate or even particularly meaningful. Faith in God was just an assumption in our family. You believe in God because my mother did and her mother did and on and on. As I look back on it now, I am grateful for being raised in a culture that had a foundation of faith, because when I needed it, my faith – however shallow and unformed - was there for me. As I have matured over the years, my faith is something that nurtures my mind and soul daily. I have a tremendous belief in an optimistic future. I believe there is a higher order to the occurrences in life, and that my life has a purpose. This belief and faith bolsters me against the inevitable winds of change.

What do you believe in? In what do you have faith? It does not have to be faith in God or a religion. You can have faith in the goodness of life, of the promise of tomorrow, or the goodness of the human race. Cultivate faith in something and you will be well on your way to mastering change.

6. Use a simple mantra. When our minds are overwhelmed with the newness of a change, at times it is hard to stay focused and grounded and to manage the emotional turmoil that comes with particularly unplanned, unwanted change. I have found at very difficult and challenging emotional times in my life, and in the lives of those I have supported in therapy, that the use of a simple mantra, repeated over and over, can bring a sense of calm and offer some self-soothing. A mantra is simply a short phrase that is repeated. It is used to calm and center the mind when it is running amok with thoughts, worries and fears. The one I use and have shared with hundreds of therapy clients over the years is the phrase, "This too shall pass." It is a phrase that immediately brings perspective to the difficulty. "This too shall pass" reminds us that nothing is permanent, that the current difficulty will end, and that eventually a new normal will be reached.

Another mantra I have often used is the simple phrase, "Peace, be still." This phrase is so simple, yet so comforting. It is a gentle reminder that peace is a thought away, and that in the ground of peace is stillness. Stillness that is full of comfort, patience and knowing that the tide will eventually turn.

Your mind is a powerful tool that can cause despair or resistance to unwanted change or can offer comfort in the midst of loss and uncertainty. Try using this phrase today when you are met with any minor irritation during your day and see if you don't immediately feel the soothing power of these simple phrases. This too shall pass. Peace, be still.

7. Operate within Your Change Temperament. While some people use a major change as impetus to reinvent their entire life, you have to address these circumstances inside of a solid understanding of your change temperament. When you are stressed and overwhelmed with an unwanted change thrust into your life, your mind is not optimally clear, your emotions are on overdrive and your psyche may leave you wanting to take flight. If you lean toward being more change averse, you definitely want to strive to keep other elements of your life consistent until you have reached the resolution stage of the change. This will only serve to make your life easier and bring you less angst. If you are a change seeker, leaning toward a total life makeover may actually help you ride the wave of change. It is a potential pitfall when facing change to think it will ease the angst of the transition period to heap on even greater change. I have seen people engage in "fight of flight" behavior when unwanted, unexpected change is thrust upon them. For example, Madeline lost her job in Silicon Valley in an unexpected downsizing of her company. She was overcome with anxiety and fear of how she would support herself despite the fact that she was given a generous severance package and could have easily lived on it for 6-8 months. Her adaptability to change was not well developed and she did not understand how to master transitions, so she packed up her things in California and moved back to live with her parents in rural Alabama rather than tolerating the anxiety, making a plan, getting some support, taking inventory of her values and what she next wanted in life. Within a few months of her move back to Alabama, Madeline realized that there was no job market in that area for someone with her technology skill set. She became even more distraught, questioning her decision-making. Having lost faith in herself and her capacity to make sound decisions, she was swallowed up in doubt and despair. After a long six months of battling anxiety, depression and losing her sense of direction, someone suggested that she hire a professional coach to help her with this next phase of decisions and life planning. To her credit, Madeline took the advice and sought coaching. Through this process, she engaged in values clarification work, looking at what she truly wanted and how she most enjoyed expressing herself. After a few months of job search, she landed a job in a rural, progressive part of the country, working at a much smaller technology startup company where she was a key player in their development. This time, when she made her move, she made a clear plan based on her values and desires to guide her and had the support of the coaching relationship to sustain her. With these structures in place, Madeline made a successful transition to the new geographic location and the new job with ease and enjoyment. Two years later, she had put down roots in this new community and felt greater confidence in her decision-making than ever before. She understood her change temperament in a new way that gave her the confidence to move forward with all the tools and support she needed to make prudent, life-affirming change.

8. Garner support. If you lose faith in yourself, a nice next best thing is to have the support of others who believe in you. I often tell my coaching and therapy clients, "If you can't believe in yourself right now, believe in my belief in you. I have enough for both of us!" Having the support of others is such a tremendously important aspect to managing change. We are relational beings and we thrive best inside of the loving energy of nurturing, compassionate, stimulating relationships. If you are having a particularly hard time adapting to a change, by all means, seek the support of a professional. A caring relationship with a minister, counselor or coach can be a tremendous catalyst for getting through the most difficult times of change. Support groups are invaluable and there is a host of social science research that points to the validity of such groups to improve one's adjustment to change. Cancer support groups have proven time and again to lengthen the life span of cancer patients. Grief support groups help decrease the amount of complicated mourning that follows the loss of a loved one. A client of mine who is a physician once engaged in a malpractice lawsuit support group, and the support she felt being with other physicians who were engaged in malpractice suits was a tremendous help in her regaining her sense of confidence and self-esteem as a practitioner. The importance of a support group or a caring, supportive professional relationship cannot be overstated.

Here is a helpful checklist that can help you know if you are in a position in life that you would benefit from a support group or from a supportive professional relationship:

☐ I often wish there were others who understood what I was going through.

☐ I just want someone to listen and not try to fix or change what I am going through.

☐ I sometimes feel embarrassed for wanting to talk about what I am going through, so I mostly just shut up about it.

☐ People really can't understand what I am going through.

☐ I enjoy talking to others people in general and getting to know people on a more personal level.

☐ It is hard to talk to those closest to me about what I am going through because I don't want them to worry or get tired of my issues.

☐ It would be nice to know other people who are going through this so I can find out if how I am feeling is crazy or just part of this process.

If you checked three or more of these statements, you would clearly benefit from some form of support for the change you are going through. The support could be in the form of a support group, or one-on-one relationship with a therapist, spiritual counselor or coach. There are vastly different approaches in all of these supportive disciplines, so it is important for you to get clear on what each one offers before engaging a provider. Asking friends for referrals and reading a bit about each discipline will help you discern the best support. Be particularly mindful if you are having difficulty sleeping, have lost your appetite or interest in things you normally enjoy, are isolating from friends and activities, or if you feel like you are "crawling out of your skin," your thoughts are going too fast or if you are having difficulty with your heart beating too fast. These are some of the symptoms of depression and anxiety and require at least a professional consultation and perhaps some ongoing treatment.

Who do you have in your life to rely upon for this type of emotional support? Who are the people to whom you know you can express yourself without fear of criticism or needing to candy-coat your emotions? If you feel that you cannot list more than one or two people, or if you cannot list any at all, it is a perfect time to explore engaging in a professional supportive relationship. I call these relationships "change agent relationships" meaning that the whole point of the relationship it so support your growth and adaptability to change.

9. Keep it simple, but keep moving. For many people dealing with unwanted change, there is a sudden feeling of inertia or immobilization due to feeling overwhelmed by the change. One day life is ticking along just fine, you are engaged with life, doing things that are yours to do and then "Wham!" a sudden, unwanted change comes your way and it all but stops you dead in your tracks (hopefully not literally so!). You all know this feeling – the inertia that comes from the shock, sadness, anger and overwhelm. Perhaps some of you are feeling that right now. What's the solution? Keep it simple, but keep moving.

My client, Yvonne, comes to mind. Yvonne was a middle-aged business executive who had the world by the reins. She was in charge, successful, fast moving and up to things in life. Then, one evening when she came home from work, her husband had packed his things and was waiting for her at the door. He looked sullen, frightened almost, as he handed her a letter, said, "I'm sorry but I am leaving," and walked out the door. Yvonne said she felt like someone shot a cannonball straight into her stomach. To her credit, she sought my coaching services within a mere six weeks of this tremendous loss. She was still somewhat in shock, angry as an agitated pit bull, but resolute to put her life back together again. She was completely immobilized, beyond knowing she needed help to get through this. So we set out a plan for each week that included simple things to keep her moving – simple things like going to work for at least part of the day, going for a ten or twenty-minute walk with a compassionate co-worker or friend, getting referrals for lawyers, interviewing a few. We focused on doing one small thing every day that was designed to combat her feeling of total immobilization, yet did not overwhelm her. We purposefully avoided the more emotionally-laden tasks of going through old pictures, clearing out her husband's "left overs" as she called them – the tools, fishing equipment and video games that were clearly his that she did not want. We focused on doing things that were moving her forward and yet were gentle enough for her to accomplish in this early phase of the loss. After a few months of this, Yvonne gained confidence and also processed the emotional elements of her loss a great deal. She was ready for bigger things, which lead to our next tool to manage and master change…

10. Reinvent yourself. Perhaps the most compelling thing about going through unexpected, unwanted change is the degree to which it allows, or forces you almost, to reinvent yourself. If you have had a significant enough shake up in life, one like those experienced by some of these stories above, it is often a huge wake up call to look deeply at the way you are living your life and make some serious adjustments. In fact, how many of you know someone who has gone through unimaginable difficulty, with an illness or a loss, who ended up saying that they are grateful for the experience because of how it impacted them or changed their life? I'm sure you all do. I do too – a former coaching client and my dear friend, Denise Desimone, is someone who used an unwanted, unplanned change as a major catalyst to reinvent her life. In 2006, Denise was diagnosed with Stage 4 neck and throat cancer. Her doctors told her to go home and get her affairs in order and gave her a few short months to live. While the doctors told her she would not live, Denise had tremendous faith in God, a powerful prayer practice, a huge loving network of family and friends and she beat those odds. Then they told her she would never speak again due to the radiation and surgery in her throat, and yet she now devotes herself full time to speaking, signing and practicing her healing arts around the country. Denise used her cancer experience to completely reinvent her life. Prior to this radical uninvited change in Denise's life, she had worked part time in the alternative and complimentary healing arts field and was also a musician and singer. But she had always pursued these parts of her life in a part time fashion, maintaining a day-job, as many people do, to pay the bills. Denise's story of recovering from her cancer diagnosis with a combination of traditional and complimentary healing strategies is a remarkable story of faith, wisdom and love. Within a year of her surgery and recovery, she was invited to sing the National Anthem at Boston's Fenway Park on the Jimmy Fund Cancer Awareness Day in front of thousands of cheering fans. You can read her inspiring story in her book, "From Stage 4 to Center Stage."

The process of *life reinvention*, or "Life Design" as I call it in my course, is perhaps the most exciting and yet challenging process you can initiate. It requires strength, courage and a good sense of inner awareness. You will want to be sure you reinvent yourself in line with your desires, not those thrust upon you by your spouse, employer or other family members. Take the time to write about what you truly want your life to be like, and then write down what changes would need to be made in order to have your life be that way, and then what you need to do to initiate those changes. The entire next section will focus on this process.

Part 2

After all of this talk about change that is thrust upon us, let's shift gears to address a much more empowering topic of intentionally choosing and creating life change. Developing your capacity around managing unexpected change bolsters your ability to design and create the changes that you long to experience.

This topic is a cumulative one – all of the elements we covered about responding to unexpected change apply to creating planned and intended change, but there are some other elements that need to be added that will enhance your effectiveness and power.

I have often told my coaching clients over the years that there is no problem that you can bring to me that I can't give you a coaching structure to address and resolve. The question is not whether there is a potential solution or structure, the question is whether or not you will implement it. There really is a formula for creating the life that you want. There are certain life laws or principles that when consistently applied will lead you toward the direction of your dreams and desires. It is not an easy way to live, but it creates the most fulfilling, engaged and contented life that I know.

And still, the process of initiating and sustaining life change is a difficult one. Human beings are a complex web of desire for and resistance to change all at the same time. Your ego is geared toward keeping things the same, which leads you to feel safer and more secure in the world. That is not a bad thing, but it is something that must be understood and managed in order to create long-lasting change. I often find that self-help books and short empowerment retreats or workshops make the process of change sound much simpler than it actually is. Perhaps you are reading this book because there is some life change you are struggling with and you are looking here for advice, direction, support and some sense of understanding your change process. What is that change? What have you tried up to this point that has worked or that didn't? Whom have you relied upon? What false assumptions did you bring to the change process? These are all important questions as you begin learning how to master creating life change.

There are some basic underlying beliefs that I bring to the change process and it would be good for you to know them and at least try them on for a while. See how these beliefs line up with your view of the world; talk these over with a friend or someone who is interested in talking more deeply about life. Allow yourself the gift of thinking deeply about your existence and purpose.

One of the underlying beliefs that inform my work is that we are all here with a purpose. In fact, one of my operating beliefs is that there is a single purpose to all of humanity; there is a reason we, the human species, are here. I believe that purpose has to do with our human evolution – where we have come from and where we are going as a species. I believe that the single purpose of humanity is to grow in our consciousness, our perspectives and world view, to ever-increasing levels of divine love, joy and oneness. It is well beyond the scope of this book to delve deeper into this subject, but for now, suffice it to say that my approach to creating sustained life change is grounded in a philosophy that includes this perspective.

My next underlying belief about the process of creating sustained change is that you are here with a unique, individual, important and compelling mission to deliver to humanity – maybe not to the entire world, but to the piece of humanity that your life touches. If you begin with the premise that all of humanity is here to grow, the next question becomes, "What is my part in that human evolutionary story?" The answer to this lies in what I call your *personal mission*. You personal mission is the thing that you came here to experience, contribute and deliver on earth. It is the reason your soul incarnated at this particular time in human history. Getting in touch with your personal mission, and even writing a personal mission statement, is a powerful personal exercise that can help guide your life and decisions from that time forward.

The next underlying belief is that as you get in touch with your personal mission and begin to align your life's actions with it, you immediately tap into a flow of energy, or consciousness, which brings greater ease and happiness to life. How you begin tapping into what your personal mission is to get in touch with the things you most love, the things that light you up, the things that make you come alive. What do you truly desire? What do you enjoy talking about or reading? What did you love to do as a child? What comes naturally to you? These are the elements that make up one's personal mission. It is not necessarily what you do for your employment, although there is often a good deal of overlap in one's mission with one's vocation. But it is more along the lines of who you are being no matter what you are doing. That's an odd notion to wrap your head around. Let me say that again – your personal mission is about who you are being no matter what you are doing.

My personal mission is, "I am a torchbearer for a vision of a world transformed, illuminating freedom, fulfillment and passion, igniting the flame of infinite possibility for the human spirit." Now, I do not possess a job where I walk around with a lit torch, lighting other people's torches! It is a metaphor for who I am – I have always been engaged with helping people to grow for as long as I can remember. Even in high school I was the class "Dear Abby" or the one that others turned to with a crisis or problems. In my senior yearbook, one of my classmates wrote, "You're a good listener no matter what the problem is. You know how to help people. Keep it up, you're good at it." And so my entire life, whether I am teaching a seminar, writing a book or just hanging out with friends, is about empowering others to live their fullest potential, to discover what they came here to be in life and then to live that to the fullest. (For

guidance on how to create your personal mission statement, go to my website at:
http://www.jackiewoodside.com/assets/Creating_Your_Personal_Mission_Statement.pdf

A. The Six Keys of Creating Sustained Change

1. Get clear on what you desire. Even if you don't engage in the work of developing your own personal mission statement, you can at least get clear on what you desire. I am often astounded when I talk with people casually that most people really do not have a sense of what they want or desire. People most often live life by default – just going along with the things that happen to come their way rather than taking charge of life and moving toward their desires. That makes sense because if you don't know what you want, it will be awfully hard to go about getting it! It seems crazy to me to go through one's entire life without ever asking the question, "What is it that I truly desire? What do I want to have my life be about? What do I want to experience and express?" To me there is nothing more fulfilling than living life with clarity, power and intention – in other words, living life by design. Therefore, *clarity* is key to creating sustained change – you have got to answer the question "What is it that I want to create?"

2. Move toward your desires. It is one thing to say that you have to get clear on what you desire, however if you get clear on it but do nothing to move toward it, then you are setting yourself up for a life of frustration! I tell my coaching clients that coaching is an action-oriented discipline, which is what I love about it. Coaching is not about thinking about change or developing insights. Insights are a dime a dozen – the important question is what are you going to DO with the insights that will make a sustained difference in your life? You have got to get engaged in the process of moving toward your desires, which is what creating sustained change is all about. How do you move toward your desires? That's the next step…

3. Create your compelling *Why*. One of the fundamental reasons people fail to institute long-lasting change is due to not establishing a context of meaning. The work I mentioned above regarding discerning your core values, and writing your personal mission and vision creates the context of meaning for you. This work is done before the specific goals are established. This is a *specific formula* that consistently generates success in the areas of desired change. Too many people establish the goal without establishing the meaning behind the goal – and then they don't succeed. Goals without meaning are mere busywork. Goals attached to a greater context of mission, vision and purpose have power and I believe even magic in them.

I have never been a fan of "motivation." I tell my coaching clients that motivation is nice when it is present, but it is who you are being and what you choose to do when you are *not* motivated that will create sustained change and leave a lasting impact on your life and likely on other's lives as well. Far too often people get confronted with the actual work to implement sustained change and simply give up. They think there is something wrong with them because they're not motivated long enough to create change. emotion. It is a fleeting response to emotionally laden input. That is the reason for needing to create a compelling *why*.

Dick Hoyt is someone who comes to mind for me when I think of someone who has done extraordinary things driven by a compelling *why*. He has run over 1000 races that have included full marathons and triathlons, even several Ironman triathlons. If this accomplishment isn't enough, then add the fact that he did each of these races while pushing his full-grown son in a wheelchair, pulling him on an inflatable boat, and riding with him in a specially designed bike seat on the front of his own bicycle. Dick's son, Rick, was born with Cerebral Palsy and as a result was never able to ambulate on his own. Dick and his wife were unrelenting advocates for their son in school and in every other facet of life. So when Rick wanted to do a road race, Dick took on the charge and the two finished a small local 5K race together, next to last! That was 35 years ago. The man is a legend in the running and triathlon community and an inspiration to millions of people around the globe. While I was writing this section of the book, I called Dick and had a lovely conversation with him about his compelling why. Here is a small portion of what he said:

Rick loved sports. He would come alive when he would watch the games or when we would go to any sporting event. After Rick learned to communicate with his communication board, he told me one day that he wanted to run a race. I had no idea how we were going to accomplish it, but I got one of those jogging strollers and pushed Rick in a local 5K. We were awful, came in next to last, but after the race, Rick told me that when he runs (in tandem with me), he feels free of his disability. He feels like he is not handicapped. After he told me that, he told me that he wanted to run a marathon and then it just kept going from there.

Dick is an example of someone who took his compelling *why* that leads him to do extraordinary things.

The changes you want to initiate may not be as profound or as challenging as what Dick and Rick Hoyt have done over the past 35 years. Regardless of the depth or scope of your desired change, you will need to face the same fears, demons, ambivalence and difficulty that the Hoyts faced. If change were easy, no one would have any complaints!

4. Create a vision for your life. Once you get clear on what you desire, do the next step and actually write it all down in a personal vision. A *personal vision* is your detailed description of what you want your life to be. It should include what you want to experience, learn, create and contribute to life and those around you. This is not to say that your life becomes a narcissistic pursuit of only that which you desire. Of course, your desires have to be discussed and created in harmony with those that you love. But this is where the magic happens – when you begin truly going within to discover that which wants to be expressed through you, it creates a certain symmetry where things have a way of lining up to clear the path for fulfillment. It really is magical and can only be fully understood when you have experienced it. It all begins with getting clear on what you value, looking to see how you want to express those values in your life, understanding that you have a personal mission that is guided by your desires, and then beginning to move toward them by aligning your actions with your values and desires.

Let me give you a personal example from my own life. When my cousin, Jeff, offered me the opportunity to purchase Aunt Kitty's cottage from him, I had no way of being able to financially afford a second home and no idea how I would make it happen. Instead of following the path of logic (saying, "No, sorry, Jeff, I don't have the money."), I followed the path of desire because I had wanted to own a home in the 1000 Islands since I left that area to go to college. So instead I said, "Sure, Jeff. I'll have to work out a few things but I'm sure I can figure it out." He then went on to tell me that I would not need to get a bank mortgage, but that I could pay him directly over any number of years that I needed to, and I could set my own terms within reason. Wow! I was floored! So already, I was well on my way to figuring out how I was going to fulfill my dream of owning a home in the Thousand Islands. But then something equally as miraculous occurred. I was fretting how I would come up with the extra money every year when a good friend of mine happened to come into town to visit me the weekend after Jeff called. When I was describing the situation to him, he immediately had a solution – and one that not only worked, but offered me financial benefit beyond what I needed (there's that magic again!). My friend, Robert and his wife, Cynthia, own two homes in Saratoga Springs and Lake Placid, NY. For years they had lived between the two homes, renting out one as a short-term vacation rental when it was not in use and living in the other. Robert looked at my home – a waterfront home 30 miles from Boston, and knew immediately that I could rent it out as a vacation rental when I was living in the islands. He showed me what web site he used, set up my account, and gave me all the paperwork I needed to start renting out my Massachusetts home when I was not there. The income that I generated from my first summer renting out my home totally covered the cost of the cottage and the property taxes as well! It all started with me being clear on the desire to live in this pristine, rural, open and expansive area for part of the year, then I created the vision for it, wrote it down, and miracles occurred. But the miracles didn't occur while I sat back and did nothing. This leads to the next step in creating sustained change.

5. Translate your vision into goals. Most often our visions do not manifest themselves without our doing something to help them along. This is where our actions must align with our desires – in other words, you most often have to *do something* in order for your vision to become a reality. For years before I got that call from my cousin, Jeff, I had told him that I wanted to buy it from him someday and we had agreed that I would have "right of first refusal" meaning he would offer it to me before putting it on the open real estate market or offering it other others in the family. If I didn't begin that conversation with Jeff, he would not have known I was interested in it and likely would not have called to see if I wanted to purchase it from him! Similarly, whatever dreams that make up your personal vision, you have got to put feet to your dreams by detailing what actions you will take to create the outcomes you desire. Goals are dreams with a deadline! They are the specific action steps that you will take to bring your desired change into manifestation. If your dream is to have a Ph.D. a reasonable first step would be to research programs, then find out the application requirements, then get your materials together and apply. If your desired change is own your own company rather than be an employee, a reasonable first step would be to start identifying your product or service and target market, developing a business plan, seeking required funding and support, and talking to others who have done what you want to do. Just this week I had a wonderful conversation with a man who is a corporate Human Resources professional. Jonathan wants to go into full time professional coaching so one of his first actions was to interview coaches who have different types of coaching practices and learn from them what the first steps might be. This is a great example of putting feet to your desired change. You've got to get into action. The action alone creates a shift in your energy and perceptions; it bolsters your confidence and feeds your enthusiasm so that you stay engaged with your change process.

6. Create accountability. I have often told my coaching clients that if I did nothing more than hold them accountable for doing what they know they should do, they would get more than their money's worth. So far none of them have disagreed with me! You know that it is true – there are so many things in life that you "know you should do" that you're not doing. What if you added in some accountability for them? What difference would that make? Jonathan not only was taking action by gathering information, he also had created ongoing accountability for himself in the form of having his own personal coach.

Accountability is a structure inside of which you deliver, on which you decide you want to do. Sports coaches hold players accountable for staying on task of goals and plans. Managers hold their teams accountable to delivering on their timelines, projects and company goals. Teachers hold students accountable for doing their schoolwork. We are incredibly acculturated toward accountability. Think about it. From a very young age, we know who it is that is in charge, keeping things in order and insuring that we do what we are supposed to do. Weight Watchers and AA or any of the 12-step programs are great accountability structures for dealing with the life issues of weight loss or addictions of any kind. I add accountability into my Life Design. Each course participant is assigned to a Personal Accountability Team (PAT) for the duration of the course. Each team holds a weekly teleconference so people are continually engaged with the coursework and the conversation for intentionally designing their lives in alignment with their values and mission. As I stated earlier, creating sustained change is an action-oriented process, so each participant is engaged in writing their core values, mission, vision and then discerning their goals and getting into action around their Life Design. This team approach creates what I call a "change agent relationship." It is a beautiful process that indeed creates long-lasting and meaningful change. The PAT group is a key component to people staying in action and actually doing the work of the course rather than keeping it in their head thinking they "should do it someday."

By creating accountability, a change agent relationship makes us successful more quickly than doing such work alone. A change agent relationship can be with a coach, AA group, support group, therapist, work out buddy or fitness instructor. The truth is change doesn't happen in a vacuum. We need to be engaged in relationships with people who support our growth and who are aligned with the notion of creating a better life. While it is important to have a trusting relationship with your accountability partner, I don't recommend using your spouse as an accountability partner. When your spouse holds you accountable, it can feel far too much like nagging! I don't recommend it! Most often it is best to use someone not too close to your daily life, which is why having a coach as your accountability partner is a steady, reliable and often deeply meaningful relationship.

B. Bring it on!

Mastering and creating intentional change is really what life is all about. It is the growth process, and I believe it is what we, as human beings, are here to do. I believe that people *want* to change for the better and deeply desire to grow. I believe you feel a yearning for greater meaning in your life, for more contribution and to know that you have made a difference. Don't allow the ideas in this book to die in your mind. Put them into practice in your life. Remember, coaching is an action-oriented discipline. Life change occurs not by thinking about it, but by *doing things differently*. Different actions produce different results. Get on it. What are you waiting for? There is never going to be a perfect time to initiate this change or to get a better handle on the change that has come your way. This is it. This is your time, your window of opportunity. You can be the one who is strong, who is making a difference, and who others remember all of their lives for the example you set by following your dreams. Start today, now! Not after dinner, or some other more convenient time. Call someone and tell him or her that you are ready to deal with this change. Then put these structures into your life. I promise you they will lead you to a better tomorrow.

Chapter Six: The Most Important Change of All

What is your greatest asset? Is it your 401K? Your well-diversified investment portfolio? Your home? Perhaps you see your stable and happy marriage as your most important asset. What determines the quality of your life? Your circumstances or family relationships? Your net worth? Your job? None of these do. It is easy to think that they do – particularly in our externally-oriented culture, but what creates the quality of your life is entirely based on the quality of your inner life. For there is nothing that has a greater impact on you than your mind and the perspective you bring to life. The externals in our lives are pleasant amusements or disdainful distractions from all that we truly need – which is a deep and abiding connection to that which is within us.

I want to describe two different people and then ask you whom you would think would be the happier, more fulfilled of the two. One is a friend of mine, a very wealthy, successful, single, athletic, middle-aged man who has close family ties, has lived in the same geographic area most of his life and is well-connected in his local community. He owns several gorgeous vacation homes, a boat and a jet ski and some nice cars. He is very intelligent and well-educated. He enjoys going to church and frequently attends social gatherings with friends and family. The other person is a young woman, a single mother with a high school education. She lives on public assistance and resides at the home of her mother's former boyfriend with whom she maintains close ties. She has two children less than three years of age from two different fathers. She is unemployed because she cannot find work that would support her and cover the cost of child care. She goes to church and has some social support from those in the congregation where she attends.

I'm certain that most people would choose the former example as being someone who is enjoying a happier, more satisfied life, but nothing could be further from the truth. My friend, Ted, while successful and gifted in so many ways, is one of the most grumbling, discontented people I know, while the young woman, Angie, carries herself with an air of contentment, peace and optimism that few display. What is the difference? Why would one with seemingly such advantageous circumstances face life with such angst and discontent while someone with such difficult life circumstances to greet each day with gratitude and positive expectancy? The answer is simple, complex, mystical and scientific all at the same time. The difference has to do with the power of the mind, or more specifically; human consciousness.

The scientific study of human consciousness is a rapidly growing field that I believe is the next frontier in the expansion of our understanding of human potential. We have yet to begin to understand what the complex possibilities latent in the human mind. It is this burgeoning field of consciousness that is leading the way to broaden our understanding. It is our level of consciousness, or our perspective on things, that gives us our experience. Period. Life truly is an inside job. The most important change you will ever learn to make is to learn to change your perspective.

If you have read this far, you have spent a good amount of time thinking about how to master life change. Perhaps you have spent additional hours in conversation about what you have been reading. You have likely opened your mind to some new ways of seeing things and that is a very good thing, because developing your capacity to see things in a new way is essential to leading a happy life. The only meaning anything has in our lives is the meaning we give it. This is almost impossible to see when we are steeped in our perceptions and interpretations, but it is fully the truth. I have seen people inherit large sums of money and relate to it as a problem, and I have seen people diagnosed with end-stage cancer and see it as a blessing. There is no "way that things are." There is only the way *that you* are. The way that you are is determined by your consciousness, or by the sum total of your perspectives on life – your unique definition of "the way life is."

Learning to change your mind, your perspective and ultimately your level of consciousness is the most important change of all. It is your path to lasting happiness and your ticket to inner peace. Fundamentally, isn't that what we all want? Accumulating wealth, nice possessions and accomplishments is great, but if you do so at the expense of your happiness and inner peace, what value does it truly bring?

The words *mind* and *brain* are often used interchangeably, but they are not the same thing. Your brain is the seat of your mind, your mind is the seat of consciousness, and your consciousness is the seat of your soul. One's consciousness is situated in every cell of the body. In fact, Candice Pert in her book "The Molecules of Emotion" indicates from her research that each cell has its own "mind" or inner intelligence.

So when you are setting out to create change in your life, you first have to create change in your mind. You literally have to change your mind about the thing. You need to develop a new perspective and set of beliefs that will support the new direction. Too many people will never do this work for it is challenging to dig deep into your current beliefs and perspectives to unearth those that no longer serve the new direction you want to take. People too often stay comfortably housed inside the bounds of their life experience, too frightened or intimidated to debunk their own myths or see beyond their own limited world view. I am sometimes tempted to envy people who live that way for it seems like a much simpler and less complicated way to live than how I barrel along, telling Life how things are going to be. But I cannot live in such narrow spaces. My mind does not want to be confined to the thoughts I have always had, the experiences that are only familiar to me. My consciousness wants to grow and expand so I bow my often frightened and disgruntled ego to the power of my mind, and flow from the tiny meadows to the expanse of mountaintops. I don't want my life to be small. I want to know the fear of expansiveness, while simultaneously living inside the joy and comfort of contentment. That is one radical way to live. Leaning into the bare bosom of Life; being happy just as and where I am, and invite Life to wrap her loving arms around me and show me how to grow.

Grow, grow, grow. This seems to be the never-ending chant from the seat of one's soul that whispers in the ear of consciousness and wafts into a symphony in the mind. When we slow down and listen the mind fills with ideas of what is possible, filtered through the lens of desire. If you can awaken and be aware of this process, then your mind can get engaged to begin taking the mere whispers of a dream and turn them into a vision, a goal, and ultimately a life intentionally lived.

If you really want to master change, develop the capacity to find the blessing in everything. As a young child, I always noticed the poignant and sometimes pained way that my grandmother, Grace, spoke about how grateful she was to have her grandchildren and what a blessing they were to her. It was not until many years later that I understood the depth of meaning this had to her. She had lost so much – her husband and two of her three sons, and yet she had her grandkids to love and nurture. She cultivated a perspective in which she found the blessing amid the immense tragedy in her life and it was this blessing that she embraced and that gave her life meaning.

If you live long enough, you too will be faced with circumstances that people will call tragic and others that people call marvelous. You will experience loss as well as success. At each circumstance, what matters more than what you are experiencing is what you are making the experience mean. There is no inherent meaning to any life circumstance, as I hope this book has helped you to see. What you decide about a thing becomes your truth and your truth gives rise to your way of being (or level of consciousness) and your way of being gives rise to the quality of your life.

Change your perspective and you change your life. It is as simple and profound as that. You are here to grow and change, and the only way you will grow as a person is to change your consciousness. Take this notion in and listen to your intuition to see if this doesn't ring true for you. Take what you have learned in this book and put it into practice in your life, even if it is just one simple thing, and watch to see how you are training yourself to master this thing called change.

Appendix A

PHYSICAL	EMOTIONAL	SPIRITUAL
Take a hot bath or sauna	Call or visit a friend	Pray
Go for a walk in nature	Have a good cry	Meditate
Engage in a gentle yoga practice	Talk to a therapist or life coach	Affirm the good in your life
Take a nap	Watch a funny movie	Attend an uplifting spiritual service
Eat something healthy and delicious	Read a good book	Give assistance to others

Appendix A

PHYSICAL	EMOTIONAL	SPIRITUAL
Take an afternoon or a day off to do nothing at all	Keep a gratitude journal of the blessings in your life	Read uplifting spiritual literature
Get a massage	Say kind things to yourself	Practice acceptance
Clean out a closet	Listen to soothing or upbeat music	Surrender your cares to the power of the universe

ABOUT THE AUTHOR

Jackie Woodside, CPC, LICSW is the founder of the Woodside Wellness Institute for the treatment of depression and anxiety. She received her Master of Social Work degree from Boston College and her professional coach certification through the Institute for Professional Excellence in Coaching. As a certified professional coach, Jackie created numerous holistically-oriented empowerment courses including Life Design, Life Mastery and Energy Management. She was a contributing author to the award-winning book, "Conscious Entrepreneurs" and is a regular contributor to the New Face of Leadership e-zine in the Coach's Corner section.

Jackie is a masterful speaker, trainer and coach specializing in helping people manage, create and adapt to change. She lives with her family between their homes in central Massachusetts and the Thousand Islands of upstate New York.

Jackie can be reached via her web site at www.JackieWoodside.com **and** at Jackie@JackieWoodside.com.

Made in the USA
Charleston, SC
13 February 2013